Classification and Diagnosis of Psychological Abnormality

How is psychological abnormality recognised? How many different mental disorders are there, and what are their characteristics? Although there are established guidelines for clinicians working in this area, these have been subject to many criticisms. Exploring how views on this subject have changed over time, and how they vary in different societies, poses important questions about our current practices.

This book provides a brief overview of the current definitions and various explanations for psychological abnormality and then focuses on how society diagnoses and classifies behaviour that is deemed to be 'unusual'. Three key areas of the topic are covered: the procedures involved in the diagnosis and classification of mental disorders (such as schizophrenia); research into the history and origins of multiple personality disorder; and a discussion of the implications of cultural variability (including culture-bound syndromes) for the classification and diagnosis of psychological abnormality.

Classification and Diagnosis of Abnormal Psychology is an introductory text suitable for students and teachers of the AQA Psychology A2 specification and is also useful for other groups who work in the field of mental disorder, such as nurses, social workers and therapists.

Sue Cave is a senior examiner and coursework moderator for A level Psychology, and a lecturer at the University of Kent.

Routledge Modular Psychology

Series editors: Cara Flanagan is a Reviser for AS and A2 level Psychology and lectures at Inverness College. Philip Banyard is Associate Senior Lecturer in Psychology at Nottingham Trent University and a Chief Examiner for AS and A2 level Psychology. Both are experienced writers.

The *Routledge Modular Psychology* series is a completely new approach to introductory-level psychology, tailor-made to the new modular style of teaching. Each short book covers a topic in more detail than any large textbook can, allowing teacher and student to select material exactly to suit any particular course or project.

The books have been written especially for those students new to higher-level study, whether at school, college or university. They include specially designed features to help with technique, such as a model essay at an average level with an examiner's comments to show how extra marks can be gained. The authors are all examiners and teachers at the introductory level.

The *Routledge Modular Psychology* texts are all user-friendly and accessible and include the following features:

- practice essays with specialist commentary to show how to achieve a higher grade;
- chapter summaries to assist with revision;
- progress and review exercises;
- glossary of key terms;
- summaries of key research;
- further reading to stimulate ongoing study and research;
- cross-referencing to other books in the series.

Also available in this series (titles listed by syllabus section):

Classification and Diagnosis of Psychological Abnormality

Susan Cave

First published 2002
by Routledge
27 Church Road, Hove, East Sussex, BN3 2FA

Simultaneously published in the USA and Canada
by Taylor & Francis Inc.,
29 West 35th Street, New York, NY 10001

Routledge is an imprint of the Taylor & Francis Group

© 2002 Psychology Press

Typeset in Times and Frutiger by Keystroke,
Jacaranda Lodge, Wolverhampton
Printed and bound in Great Britain
by TJ International Ltd, Padstow, Cornwall

Cover design by Terry Foley

British Library Cataloguing in Publication Data
A catalogue record for this book is available from the British Library

Library of Congress Cataloging-in-Publication Data
Cave, Susan, 1949–
Classification and diagnosis of psychological abnormality / Susan Cave.
p. ; cm. – (Routledge modular psychology series)
Includes bibliographical references and index.
1. Mental illness–Classification. 2. Mental illnes–Diagnosis. I. Title.
II. Routledge modular psychology.
[DNLM: 1. Mental Disorders–diagnosis. 2. Mental Disorders–classification.
WM 141 C378s 2002]
RC455.2.C4 C385 2002
616.89–dc21   2001048729

ISBN 0-415-23101-9 (hbk)
ISBN 0-415-23102-7 (pbk)

Contents

Illustrations

Figures

Tables

Preface

This book aims to draw attention to some of the controversial issues surrounding the way that we, as a society, deal with unusual behaviour. The assumptions that there are spontaneously arising problems, which would be seen as problematic universally, can be challenged on the basis of the material presented in this book. Variation in response at different points in time, in different cultures, and to different individuals within a culture, have all been acknowledged for a long time now. The basis of these differences needs to be explored thoroughly, as a result of which they can either be ironed out or incorporated into practice in a rational way, as appropriate.

The book begins by looking at how mental disorder has been defined, and at the different models (or approaches) to dealing with it. Chapter 2 is devoted to a description of the classification systems in current use, the categories they use and the assessment tools used in diagnosis. These are then evaluated in terms of reliability and validity, and the practical and ethical issues involved in their use. Chapters 3 and 4 take up the issues of variation over time and across cultures by looking at and evaluating research into multiple personality disorder and culture-bound syndromes. Whether or not these phenomena are genuine is discussed. Chapter 5 focuses on conclusions and implications for practice in this field. In Chapter 6 there is a selection of summarised key papers and sample student essays, complete with examiner's comments.

Definitions of terms given in bold type can be found in the glossary.

Acknowledgements

There are several writers who have persevered with their ground-breaking work in this area, sometimes in the face of a great deal of opposition, and sometimes unrecognised. Among them are David Pilgrim, Joan Busfield, Suman Fernando and Ian Hacking. All, in different ways, have worked long and hard to achieve a more equitable and reasoned approach to the kinds of issues that we are dealing with here, and they all deserve our thanks.

1

Introduction

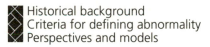

Historical background
Criteria for defining abnormality
Perspectives and models

Historical background

Prehistory and evil spirits

Some form of psychological abnormality has always been recognised. In prehistoric times the evidence that survives suggests that such behaviour was generally attributed to evil spirits. Evidence exists of exorcisms being carried out, and skulls have been retrieved that have neat holes in them. These may have been drilled to allow the evil spirits to escape – a procedure still carried out by some groups today in order to achieve heightened awareness, and known as trephining (or trepanning). It has been argued, however, that the holes discovered are more likely to be healed-over injuries (Maher & Maher 1985). This is because most of the skulls are male, and the holes are in a variety of different sites on the skull, suggesting that deliberate placement did not occur.

Ancient Greece and medical explanations

The philosopher Plato, in the 4th century BC, distinguished natural madness, resulting from physical disease, from that given by divine gift. He insisted that mental disturbance should be treated within the family, which led to special temples being set aside as retreats for the mentally ill.

Hippocrates, a Greek physician writing at the same time (often considered to be the father of modern medicine), described five forms of madness (hysteria, epilepsy, acute mental disturbance with and without fever, and chronic mental disturbance), all of which he considered to be medical in origin and treatable by procedures such as emetics, bleeding, purges and dietary change. These procedures were aiming to reduce the excess of bodily fluids, or humours, which Hippocrates thought were responsible for mental disorder. An excess of black bile was thought to lead to depression (melancholy); an excess of yellow bile to irritability and anxiety (choleric); an excess of phlegm to indifference (phlegmatic); and an excess of blood to mood shifts (sanguinity). Thus some of the modern categories of disorder had clearly been identified even then.

The Greek physician Galen, in the 1st/2nd century AD, studied anatomy in his search for explanations, but is often considered to be the first person to suggest that abnormal behaviour could also have psychological origins (Halgin & Whitbourne 1993).

The Middle Ages and demonology

By the Middle Ages (500–1500) the demonological view had taken over in Europe, and madness again became linked with possession by evil spirits. This represented a reversion to earlier ideas about evil spirits, but the ideas had been embedded in the context of Christianity. Such individuals were more likely to be subjected to exorcism or burnt at the stake than treated medically. The Inquisition was an institution set up by the Roman Catholic Church to discover and suppress heretics (those people who held opinions opposed to those of the church). In 1484, the Inquisition began in earnest with the publication of the *Malleus Malleficorum*, the witchhunter's guide to diagnosing witches. This was one of the first books to be printed and widely circulated. According to Spanos (1978) as many as 100,000 persons were dealt with in this way between 1450–1600. Not all were mentally disordered of course (many were eliminated as the result of political or economic rivalry), but it is likely that many would have been.

However, at about the same time there was also the first attempt to provide secure places for mentally disordered persons. Until this time lunatics (as they were generally known) had either been accommodated by their own families or simply cast out to fend for themselves. Bethlem hospital, opened to lunatics in London in 1403, was the first in Europe, and it was followed by another in Spain in 1408, in North America in 1639 and France in 1657.

These two views of madness, as disease or as demonic possession, continued to conflict for many centuries; only recently has the latter approach been replaced by a broader, 'moral' view of such behaviour that is less reliant on religion.

The 'Age of Reason' and moral treatment

During this period in history, science and rationality were believed to hold the key to making progress with solving human problems. Hence it has become known as the Age of Reason. Physical treatments, based on 'scientific' principles and administered by physicians, gradually gave way to moral treatment based on rational argument.

In the early 18th century lunacy was regarded as an illness, and following the Poor Laws of the late 17th century, lunatics were to be protected in asylums. As these asylums became more and more overcrowded, however, the use of chains and restraints increased. By the late 18th century, as the 'Age of Reason' prevailed, religious fervour had cooled off, and the inadequacy of physical treatments had also been recognised. There were several reasons for the latter. First, physical treatments such as the whirling chair had proved ineffective. (This was a device into which patients were strapped and rotated at speed, allegedly until blood ran from their ears.) Second, in the Bethlem scandal of 1814 it was discovered that a patient called James Norris had been kept in irons for 10 years for attacking his 'keeper'. (As usual, of course, it has been noted that there were two versions of this scandal – that Norris was an extremely violent patient, and that when chained he was kept supplied with reading materials and even had a pet cat. Nevertheless, the case roused public opinion against the use of chains in asylums, especially when such neglect was found to be common).

Third, the madness of King George III (noted in letters dated 1788) had failed to respond to the available medical treatments of bleeding, blistering and purging. His problem turned out to be porphyria, a hereditary disease that produces abdominal pain and mental confusion. At the time, it was unrecognised.

The rejection of the religious and medical approaches to dealing with mental disorder led to a third response to abnormal behaviour; the moral approach. This is considered to have originated with Francis Willis, a clergyman who was called in to treat George III. He placed great emphasis on physical remedies such as diet, exercise, physical restraint (using chairs or straitjackets) when required, and lectures on morality designed to make the patient see the error of his ways. The importance of this is that madness no longer appears to be considered to be purely physical or demonological in its origins. It is also possible, of course, that the use of different treatments does not necessarily indicate a shift in ideas about the origins of mental disorder.

The moral approach was also reflected by Chiarugi in Florence, Italy in 1788. He removed all restraints from patients and provided them with activities to occupy them. This could be considered to be the start of occupational therapy. In the Bicetre hospital in Paris, the superintendent of the incurables ward, a layman called Pussin, had similarly unchained patients and forbidden staff to beat them in 1784. He extended these reforms with the aid of Pinel, who was appointed physician in 1793 (and generally gets the credit for the improvements).

In England, the Quaker William Tuke (1732–1822) opened the York Retreat in 1796, which proved to be highly successful. It was based on moral therapy, an attempt at resocialisation that emphasised kindliness, orderliness and occupation. No physicians were employed there, and restraint was used only if absolutely necessary. The term 'moral insanity' was coined by the Englishman Pritchard in 1835 to refer to people who do not live in acceptable ways. It has been suggested (Masson 1988) that this was subsequently used as a convenient excuse to incarcerate unwanted relatives, particularly women who had an inheritance coming to them.

This conflict between the moral and the medical approaches replaced the earlier conflict between the religious and the medical approaches. This diversity can still be seen today in the different therapeutic approaches to mental disorder (see *Therapeutic Approaches in Psychology* by Susan Cave in the series).

In response to these developments, Parliament passed legislation in 1808 regarding care for the insane, but it was not until the Lunatics Act of 1845 that it became mandatory to provide asylums. These were considered to be centres for cure rather than restraint. Prior to that, many mentally disordered individuals were incarcerated in prisons or the workhouse if they couldn't afford private care. In America, the physician Benjamin Rush (1745–1813) devoted his career to the study of mental problems, and the reformer Dorothea Dix (1802–1887) campaigned for special humane facilities to be provided for the mentally ill, raising sufficient funds to found 32 mental hospitals.

The modern era and mental illness

Considerable expansion in provision occurred between 1860–1900, and the medical view prevailed once again. The first textbook of psychiatry was published by Kraepelin in 1885, and established abnormal behaviour as a manifestation of mental illness, a physical disease or dysfunction in the individual that should therefore be treated by physical means. To some extent this optimism was lost subsequently, as the asylums became more and more overcrowded and madness became regarded as incurable.

Another pioneer from this period was Freud, who studied hysteria with the neurologist Charcot in Paris. **Hypnosis** had had some popularity as a treatment for mental problems since it was first introduced by Mesmer some years before in the guise of mesmerism. Freud used it briefly, but then rejected it and developed his own system. Known as psychoanalysis, it was the forerunner of modern psychotherapies, and also reinforced the view that mental illness was curable and need not necessarily be medical in origin.

After World War II (1939–1945), the hospital population reduced again with the advent of drug treatments. The neuroleptics (major tranquillisers) in particular produced a major revolution in treatment and a liberalisation of care. Medicated patients were much better equipped to deal with everyday activities, and many could remain in the community. From the 1950s onwards, with the social psychiatry movement gaining ground, hospitalisation came to be seen as an inappropriate way to deal with the problem of mental disorder. The World Health Organisation adopted the label 'mental disorder' to replace the term 'mental illness', emphasising the fact that a physical basis had not been found for many of the conditions involved. As a result of this, and the requirement in the Mental Health Act of 1959 and the Community Care Act of 1990 for local authorities to provide more community services, many mental hospitals have now closed.

Underpinning these responses to abnormal behaviour, Halgin and Whitbourne (1993) have identified three different explanations for that type of behaviour: mystical; scientific; humanitarian. These are equivalent to the religious, medical and moral views identified earlier. The mystical view is that it results from demonic possession; the scientific view is that it results from biological factors such as faulty genes or brain disease, or psychological factors such as learning or stress; the humanitarian view is that it results from social conditions. Treatments have broadly speaking been either 'medical' or moral/religious, illustrating physical and mental (psychological) approaches, respectively. What is interesting here is the similarity in the way that mental disorder has been dealt with over time. Although the approaches have been reframed according to prevailing societal values (e.g. religious/moral) they have remained much the same for centuries.

Although a detailed discussion of the explanations for abnormal behaviour is not the aim of this book, it is important to understand that there are differences and similarities in the ways in which society as a whole, and hence the mental health professionals, have responded to abnormal behaviour. These are apparent in the attempts to define and classify (see Chapter 2), and in the different models used to understand abnormal behaviour, which we will be discussing in the rest of this chapter. Finally, most of what has been written about the history of mental disorder has focused on the way in which society has varied in its treatment of those whom it has labelled as abnormal. A more difficult issue to address is whether there has been any real change in the nature of the behaviours that evoke such labels. Would the same people have been considered abnormal today and in prehistoric times, for example? This is something to bear in mind as you read the rest of this text.

Criteria for defining abnormality

As indicated earlier, any discussions in this area depend on the existence of an agreed definition of what constitutes abnormal behaviour. Such a definition should ideally be able to cover all behaviours that are generally agreed to be abnormal; should exclude all normal behaviours;

should provide a basis for objective measurement of behaviour; and should be applicable to everyone irrespective of culture. Measurement is dealt with in more detail in Chapter 2, and culture in Chapter 4. Here we are concerned primarily with the selection of behaviours to be included in a set of criteria for mental disorder.

Ask a sample of people (about six should do) from different backgrounds what types of behaviour they would regard as abnormal. Then ask them which of those behaviours are criminal (bad) and which are 'mad'. What types of behaviour have they identified? How much agreement is there? Is there an overlap between 'mad' and 'bad'? How can they be distinguished?

Progress exercise

Legal criteria

It might be thought that the legal system, which is responsible for making compulsory treatment orders for those who display abnormal behaviour, would have agreed a suitable definition. The law differs in different countries; in Britain the 1983 Mental Health Act offers the following definition of mental disorder: 'Mental illness, arrested or incomplete development of mind, psychopathic disorder and <u>any other disorder or disability of mind</u>.'

Mental illness is not defined further, but is left up to the judgement of the professionals involved in treating such disorders. The underlined statement is similarly vague. 'Arrested or incomplete development of mind' is further defined as a state 'which includes severe/significant impairment of intelligence and social functioning and is associated with abnormally aggressive or seriously irresponsible conduct on the part of the person concerned.' Psychopathic disorder is 'a persistent disorder of, or disability of mind (whether or not including significant impairment of intelligence) which results in abnormally aggressive or seriously irresponsible conduct on the part of the person concerned.'

Some of these definitions give indications of the kinds of behaviours that are regarded as troublesome – impaired intelligence (though not always); impaired social functioning; abnormally aggressive and seriously irresponsible behaviours. However, the qualifiers (impaired, abnormally, seriously) leave a great deal of scope for subjective judgement. What is judged to be impaired social functioning by one person may be considered acceptable by another. Consider regular bouts of excessive drinking, for example.

In the light of the legal criteria, consider what level of intelligence you think constitutes 'severe/significant impairment'. Is it an IQ of 50, or 75 for example?

What is ' abnormal' aggression, and what is normal aggression? Does it have to involve physical violence, and if so to what degree? When *is* aggression justified?

What is 'seriously irresponsible conduct'? Should it include such behaviours as being seriously in debt? Not paying maintenance for children? Using 'dirty tricks' to eliminate business rivals?

Statistical criteria

In an attempt to address some of the issues raised earlier, statistical criteria have been introduced for some behaviours, based on the **normal distribution curve** (see Figure 1.1). If the mean score of the population on any given measure of behaviour is known, together with the average variation from that mean (known as the standard deviation) it is possible to identify mathematically which scores would be achieved by only a small proportion of the populace. These could then be regarded as abnormal. For example, given that the population mean score for IQ is 100, and the standard deviation (a measure of the average deviation from the mean) is 15, it could be argued that an IQ score of below 70 is abnormal, since it will only be obtained by about 2% of the population.

This system has the advantage of objectivity, in the sense that categorising the individual is done solely on the basis of the test score, without recourse to the clinician's judgement. There are also difficulties, however. First, the clinician must still decide which behaviours to measure in the first place, and exactly where to place the cut-off point, i.e. how much deviation is acceptable. Another problem is that population means may not exist for many behaviours that are thought to be relevant, such as irresponsible behaviour. It has also been shown (Robins et al., 1984, for example) that many mental disorders are

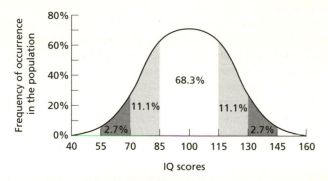

Figure 1.1 **The normal distribution curve**

statistically quite common. Approximately ⅓ of Americans will suffer from some form of mental disorder at some stage of their lives. In Britain, the lifetime prevalence for mood disorders is 15% (Harrison et al., 1998), and for women in inner London this rises to 70% for depression alone (Bebbington et al., 1989). The final weakness of the statistical criterion is that it is value-free (in theory, if not in practice). There are many people who differ from the average in ways that are considered desirable; members of Mensa, for example, would probably take exception to being labelled as abnormal, and generally they are labelled in this way. This means that as well as being statistically rare, the behaviour concerned must be regarded as undesirable; a value judgement is made.

Deviation-from-the-norm criteria

This approach takes the population norm, rather than the average, as the starting point for determining abnormality. What is important is whether the individual differs from *expected* ways of behaving. Thus depression, which is statistically quite common, would be regarded as abnormal because it is not expected of us (except in particular situations such as bereavement, and then only for a certain period of time).

The problem here is that norms differ according to culture, and even within cultures or groups at different times, as we shall see in Chapter 4. In some societies, such as the Zulu for example, hallucinations or screaming in the street are regarded as normal behaviour.

Landrine (1991) has identified a syndrome known as 'drapetomania', which used to be an acknowledged disorder in America. It was the tendency of slaves to run away from their masters. Homosexuality is a good example of a behaviour that is no longer generally regarded as abnormal in our society, and has always been perfectly acceptable in other cultures such as the Mohave Indian (Gross 1992).

According to some writers (such as Szasz 1971) such an insistence on adherence to the norm could be used to justify persecution of minority groups. Soviet Russia, for example, has been accused of treating political dissidents as if they were mentally disordered. Drapetomania can clearly be seen as a syndrome that serves the aims of one social group who wish to oppress another.

Progress exercise

Consider the positive and negative outcomes of insisting on adherence to social norms.

Mental health criteria

Jahoda (1958) proposed a set of criteria for mental health. Rather than focusing on undesirable behaviours, like the other approaches discussed here, this is a list of desirable characteristics and behaviours. Abnormality could be indicated by their absence. These criteria are as follows:

1. The absence of mental illness.
2. Being able to introspect about yourself, being aware of what you are doing and why.
3. Growth, development and self-actualisation (achievement of potential).
4. Integration of different aspects of the person (e.g. a balance between id, ego and superego in Freudian theory).
5. The ability to cope with stress.

6. Autonomy – being able to function independently.
7. Seeing the world as it really is.
8. Environmental mastery – adaptability to change, and the ability to love, work, play and have satisfactory relationships.

This is a useful way of identifying those people who would benfit from psychological help. However, it is in many ways just as prescriptive an approach as those outlined earlier, and has the additional problem that most of us would probably fail to meet all of these criteria. Many may be present to some extent, so the issues of cut-off points and difficulties with measurement also arise. Cultural variation may also be a problem. For example, collectivist societies do not value autonomy in the same way that Western, individualist societies do. They place more emphasis on family and community values and social co-operation.

Psychological and social criteria

Rosenhan and Seligman (1984) have produced a list of undesirable behaviours, and argue that if several of these exist at any one time the individual may be considered to be in need of help. The list includes such things as suffering, personal and social maladaptiveness, unpredictability and loss of control, unconventionality and irrationality, observer discomfort, and violation of moral and ideal standards. These criteria benefit from the inclusion of personal suffering, so that judgement about the individual is not solely based on the responses of other people. However, many of the criteria mentioned are difficult to measure and therefore leave a great deal to the subjective judgement of the clinician. Suffering and unconventionality are good examples.

Individual objections can be raised against the behaviours listed as well. Suffering, for example, is not always apparent. Some mentally disordered individuals (such as those who have some types of personality disorder) do not suffer themselves, although they may upset others. Unconventional behaviour may be displayed by nonconformists as well as those who are mentally disordered. Refusal to wear clothes in public places is a good recent example of this. Irrational behaviour is also not uncommon in some circumstances – if people are worried or physically ill, their behaviour may appear irrational to others. Finally, observer discomfort will vary with the observer and with the culture concerned.

The four Ds

Comer (1998) has suggested that what many of the above systems have in common can be covered by just four points:

- deviance (different, extreme behaviours such as severe depression, sexual deviance, etc.);
- distress (behaviours that upset the individual concerned, e.g. paranoia);
- dysfunctional (behaviours that interfere with everyday functioning, e.g. substance abuse, agoraphobia);
- dangerous (potentially damaging behaviours, e.g. aggression, eating disorders).

Although these seem to cover a wide range of problems, they are still not universally applicable. Some behaviours fulfil these criteria but are nevertheless acceptable; for example, the alcohol consumption of many students may be regarded as extreme, causes them distress and dysfunction, and could be dangerous. However, it is regarded as acceptable for this group of individuals, at this stage in their lives. Thus the context, as well as the content, of the behaviour must be considered.

Mental illness criteria

In this approach, abnormal behaviour is defined by the presence of particular clusters of symptoms. These symptom clusters are thought to indicate the presence of an underlying mental illness that may respond to treatment. The symptom clusters are laid down in the diagnostic and classification system current at the time. For example, the *Diagnostic and Statistical Manual of Mental Disorders* (APA 1994, 4th edition) defines mental disorder as:

a clinically significant behaviour or psychological syndrome or pattern that occurs in a person and that is associated with present distress (a painful symptom), disability (impairment in one or more important areas of functioning), a significantly increased risk of suffering death, pain, disability or an important loss of freedom. In addition, this syndrome or pattern must not be merely an expectable response to a particular event such as, for example, the death of a loved one.

The other main classification system is the International Classification of Diseases (WHO 1992, 10th edition), which defines mental disorder as 'the existence of a clinically recognisable set of symptoms or behaviours associated in most cases with distress and with interference with personal functions'. Like DSM, this focuses on the distress experienced by the individual concerned, rather than other people, and mentions symptom clusters. These classification systems will be discussed in detail in Chapter 2.

In clinical practice, use of the mental illness criteria is the favoured approach. It is clear from what has been said that the identification of symptom clusters is the critical issue here. Can they be reliably identified? Do different clinicians agree on their judgements? If they can, it still remains to be seen whether or not those clusters appear to be valid, in the sense of distinguishing syndromes that have different causes and respond to different treatments. The symptom clusters, their **validity** and **reliability** will be dealt with further in the remainder of the book.

Validity and reliability aside, there are other criticisms of this approach. Most of these are based on the argument that in many cases of mental disorder there appears to be no organic basis for the problem. Discussion of this argument in depth is beyond the brief of this text, and the reader is referred to *Psychopathology* by Stirling and Hellewell in the series. However, more and more evidence is accumulating about the physiological problems (based on genetics, brain dysfunction and biochemistry) associated with mental disorders. The difficulty for researchers is establishing whether these problems are the cause of the disorder or a consequence of it.

Another perspective on this is provided by Thomas Szasz (1960). In an article entitled 'The myth of mental illness' he made the point that the mind itself is non-physical and therefore cannot suffer from illness. His view is that mental disorder is the result of 'problems in living', which may be simply exacerbated by the use of psychiatric labels such as 'schizophrenic'. These labels are stigmatising, and may also be self-handicapping in so far as they remove the responsibility for behaviour from the individual concerned; the 'illness' can be blamed instead, and responsibility delegated to medical professionals.

Perspectives on abnormality

Before moving on to develop these issues further, we are going to look at some theoretical aspects of the topic. These underpin much of the discussion that will take place in the remainder of the text, and we will return to them in Chapter 5. Perspectives are addressed in detail in the book Theoretical Approaches in Psychology in the series. In the AQA specification, the perspectives section is divided into issues, debates and approaches. The following sections use the same structure.

Issues

The AQA specification mentions four issues that should be considered when studying any area of psychology. Here, we will briefly consider their relevance to the study of abnormality.

The first issue is gender bias. Within our society, males and females have traditionally been considered to have different roles, with the female being the dependent, nurturing homemaker and the male the independent, assertive, worker. These roles dictate how the two sexes relate to one another as well as to the world in general. When it comes to abnormal behaviour, it is perhaps not surprising that behaviours that are considered abnormal for one gender are considered to be acceptable for the other. Dependency in women, for example, is much less likely to be seen as problematic than when it is displayed in men. What may be less obvious, however, is the perpetuation of such biases in the behaviour of clinicians. Bias has been detected in the classification systems for mental disorder, and in the diagnoses and treatments given by clinicians.

Another form of gender bias can be seen in the different rates of certain mental disorders in the two sexes. Depression, as already noted, is very much more common in women than in men. There are likely to be several reasons for this, including the possibility that the different gender roles are responsible. Powerlessness and helplessness, as we shall see, are thought to be key factors in the development of some disorders, depression in particular.

The second issue is cultural bias. We have already seen that different societies have different expectations for the behaviour of their members. Looking at behaviour purely from the perspective of one society or culture will therefore provide a biased view. What is defined as abnormal in one culture will not be regarded as exceptional in another, so any criteria for defining abnormality that fail to take this into account can be described as culture-bound. A related difficulty is raised by the debate about culture-bound syndromes. These are disorders that are seen in some cultures but are not recognised in others. Anorexia nervosa, for example, may well come into this category. Whether these result from different social conditions (such as the Western emphasis on thinness in women) or whether they represent diagnostic bias is an important issue. A weaker form of the culture-bound syndrome may be evident in the different ways that disorders show themselves in different cultures. For example, depression is more likely to be associated with somatic symptoms such as digestive complaints in some cultures.

When members of other cultural groups live in a Western society, these biases become all the more evident. If certain cultural groups seem to receive particular diagnoses and treatments more frequently than other groups, we have to consider whether this is due to bias in the classification system, bias in the clinician, or differences in social conditions and pressures.

The third issue is ethics. This is the debate about what is considered right and wrong in the way that we treat one another. Clearly, when we are diagnosing mental disorder this can have profound consequences for the individual concerned. This can be considered not only in terms of treatment but also such aspects of everyday functioning as family life, housing and employment. The diagnostic label can affect the individual's self-concept (how the person sees himself or herself), usually in a negative way. This negative evaluation may well be reinforced by feedback from others, since the public stereotype of those with mental disorder is not a good one. Legal issues may also enter into this, since a diagnosis of mental disorder can provide grounds for not standing trial for crimes, or for not being held responsible for actions.

As we noted earlier, psychiatric diagnoses may also be used deliberately to dispose of unwanted persons, for either personal or political gain. This also constitutes a contravention of ethical standards.

The fourth issue is the use of non-human animals in research. Concerns here are divided into practical (whether it is admissible to extrapolate from animals to human behaviour, for example) and ethical (whether it is acceptable to use non-human animals for research purposes). Where mental disorder is concerned, this issue relates most obviously to research into the causes of mental disorders, which is not the main concern of this text (see *Psychopathology* by Stirling and Hellewell in the series). However, some of the approaches/models to be discussed in the final part of this section obviously have their roots in theories that are based on animal research. The behaviourist and biological/medical approaches are obvious examples.

Debates

Again, we will look here at the four debates mentioned in the AQA specification. These are: free will and determinism; reductionism; psychology as a science; the nature–nurture debate.

Free will and **determinism** is a discussion about the origins of our behaviour. As the term implies, the free will view is that we choose to act the way that we do. We are free agents and can make our own choices in life. This is a view espoused by the humanistic psychologists (see later). Determinism is the view that our behaviour is preset by forces outside our control, including genetics and other biological factors, past learning and experiences, and social pressures. This view is advocated by the behaviourist, psychodynamic and biological approaches, for example. A compromise position is that of soft determinism, which states that behaviour is neither totally free nor totally determined. We are predictable, but do have the option to behave in unpredictable ways. It may be unlikely that we will choose to stay in bed when we are not ill, for example, but we could if we chose to do so.

The relevance of this debate here is that mentally disordered people are often considered not to be in control of their behaviour – that is, they cannot exercise free will. Substance abusers cannot kick the habit, obsessive-compulsives cannot stop carrying out their rituals, and bulimics cannot stop bingeing. This is at the root of the legal view that mentally disordered persons are not responsible for their crimes. Some writers have also objected to the diagnostic process on the grounds that attaching psychiatric labels to people makes them somehow less responsible for their behaviour by providing an excuse. This can then be counterproductive, because they do not feel sufficiently in control to change the way that they behave.

Reductionism is the view that explanations for behaviour can be offered at several different levels, such as biological and social for example. Of these, the biological is considered by reductionists to be superior. Again, explanations for mental disorder are not really the focus of this text, but the different approaches that we will outline in the next section clearly relate to this debate. In this area, perhaps more than any other in psychology, it is important to emphasise that focusing on one level exclusively is unlikely to be a profitable approach. As the models show, multiple causes are involved in most mental disorders, and multiple treatments may also be required. Social problems (e.g. inadequate social skills) will require a different treatment from biological problems such as an imbalance in neurotransmitters (the chemicals involved in communication in the nervous system). For this reason, an eclectic approach, taking note of all aspects of the problem, is generally advocated.

Science underpins the work of psychologists in all spheres, and mental disorder is no exception to this. One key feature of the scientific approach is classification, which is the central concern of this book. Another is building theoretical explanations for mental disorder, and testing hypotheses derived from those theories through experimentation or other acceptable scientific methods. In both cases the concern is with achieving objectivity and eliminating sources of subjective bias. Throughout the following chapters we will be looking at the classification system, the process of assessment and **diagnosis**, and at specific categories such as Multiple Personality Disorder. The aim will be to evaluate them in terms of their scientific standing, particularly regarding the important criteria of validity and reliability.

Another element of the scientific approach that you may wish to consider is predictability. Science assumes that we are predictable, and that in turn implies that our behaviour is determined (see earlier). However, some allowance is made for free will, in the sense that science deals in probabilities rather than certainties. Some psychologists, notably those who espouse the humanistic approach, argue that the scientific approach is not justified in psychology. This is partly because they consider that we do have free will, and partly because they feel that subjectivity (understanding what others are experiencing) is more important than objectivity.

The **nature–nurture debate** is taken up in the realm of mental disorder by arguments about the origins of mental problems – are they present at birth (nature) or are they acquired through experience (nurture)? The interactionist position is a compromise between these two, suggesting that both are involved. This is dealt with in *Psychopathology* by Stirling and Hellewell of the series in detail, but there are some aspects that can be considered here. Perhaps the most important is the extent to which research into this topic is dependent on a reliable and valid classification system. In order to carry out research into the causes of problems such as schizophrenia, we must be able to identify schizophrenics accurately in the first place. Another important point that can be illustrated well using material from this text is the great variety of influences, both nature and nurture, which can be involved in bringing about mental disorder. This links well with the levels of analysis mentioned earlier when discussing reductionism. Cultural, social, cognitive, genetic and biochemical levels (among others) can all be seen at work in the field of mental disorder.

Approaches/models

Within psychology there are several different approaches, or **models**, which can be applied to abnormal behaviour. These determine which behaviours are regarded as abnormal, as well as how those behaviours are explained and treated, hence they have considerable practical importance. In this book we will be focusing primarily on the first of these areas, the others being dealt with by other books in this series (see *Psychopathology* by Stirling and Hellewell for explanations, and *Therapeutic Approaches in Psychology* by Susan Cave for treatments). The models we will be outlining include the biological/ medical, psychodynamic, behavioural and cognitive (as mentioned in the first part of the AQA specification), the **social constructionist**, humanistic and evolutionary (from the second part of the specification), and the family systems and socio-cultural (from the third part of the specification). The approaches underlying these models should already be familiar to AQA students. As this topic is dealt with in *Psychopathology* by Stirling and Hellewell, only a brief outline of each will be given, and an example of an explanation for mental disorder.

The medical (or biomedical) model

This approach assumes, as outlined earlier in the chapter, that abnormal behaviour exists when there is an identifiable cluster of symptoms. This cluster is indicative of an underlying physical illness, possibly involving neurological or biochemical malfunction due to genetic abnormalities, accident or disease. A biomedical explanation for depression, for example, would suggest that it may be the result of a faulty gene, a hormone imbalance, or a disorder in the system of neurotransmitters that brings about communication in the nervous system. Treatment should therefore be based on the removal of this underlying physical illness, under the direction of a physician. If it cannot be cured (e.g. by surgery), then it can be controlled by physical means using drugs or electroconvulsive shock therapy (ECT). Depression is likely to be treated using antidepressant drugs and ECT, for example.

In support of this model, it is possible to carry out scientific research to test hypotheses about medical bases for disorders. (This contrasts it with the psychodynamic model, to be discussed shortly.) Research has found support for organic involvement in some disorders. General Paresis of the Insane (GPI), for example, is known to be caused by infection with syphilis. Manic depression seems to be influenced by genes, and schizophrenics have shown abnormalities when subjected to brain scans. Physical treatments, such as drugs, have been successful in dealing with the symptoms of some disorders.

However, not all disorders have shown links with biological causes; nor is it certain that the organic changes observed in patients are causes rather than effects of the disorder. Physical treatments are by no means always successful, which again raises questions about the alleged physical basis for the disorders. We will return to this when discussing the validity of the classification systems.

The psychodynamic model

Based on the work of Freud, the view here is that we are all abnormal to some degree as a result of the inevitable clash between our innate instincts (represented by a part of the personality called the 'id') and the demands of society (represented by the 'superego'). In particular, sexual desires and the way that they are dealt with in the course of development can lead to conflicts in the unconscious mind. Although we may be unaware of these conflicts, they can have a powerful influence on our behaviour. Mediating between the id and the superego is a third part of the personality, the ego. The ego may experience anxiety as a result of pressures from these other elements of the personality. It has a variety of defence mechanisms (such as repressing distressing thoughts into the unconscious mind) that it can deploy to protect itself from this anxiety. It is the strength of the ego and its defence mechanisms that determines whether or not we will experience mental problems. In this view, depression has been considered to be the result of the early loss of a parent. This loss may be objective (as in bereavement) or subjective (if the individual feels let down or abandoned, for example). In both cases, the anger felt at the parent for leaving has been suppressed and turned on the self.

Developing the ego's capacity to deal with conflict lies at the heart of the psychodynamic approach to treatment. This entails finding out about the client's early childhood experiences, and unearthing the resultant conflicts that reside in the unconscious (such as early loss in the case of depression). In the course of psychoanalysis the analyst provides insight to the client based on the client's free associations, analysis of dreams, and on the nature of the relationship that develops between analyst and client. In the case of depression, it may involve providing a parent–child relationship in therapy, so that the individual can experience caring and understanding from another.

This approach has been very influential, but the lack of scientific basis in the way that Freud operated has led to a great deal of criticism. The theories have been based on the case study method, which focuses on individuals. This means that generalising to the population as a whole is difficult to do. Some writers (e.g. Masson 1988) have criticised Freud for being biased in the way that he dealt with patients and wrote up the cases. Furthermore, because the unconscious remains generally inaccessible, it is difficult to put Freudian concepts to the test in scientifically acceptable ways. The psychoanalytic treatment that has been developed from these ideas appears in general to be limited in the range of disorders to which it can be successfully applied. It is much more useful with less severe disorders such as generalised anxiety than with schizophrenia, for example.

The behavioural model

The behaviourists as a group (e.g. Skinner 1938) identified the study of observable behaviour to be the main aim of psychology in general. Not surprisingly, they see abnormality as being the demonstration of maladaptive behaviours. These behaviours they consider to have been learnt through conditioning processes, either operant (learning through reinforcement and punishment) or classical (learning through association). Anybody could learn these behaviours, given the appropriate environmental conditions.

In this view, depression may be a manifestation of **learned helplessness** (Seligman 1973). This is a state of apathy that results when an animal cannot escape from an unpleasant situation. It has been demonstrated in animals who are faced with aversive stimulation (such as electric shocks) from which they cannot escape. When confronted with further shocks from which they can escape, they do not do so, and the behaviours they display appear similar in some ways to those of depressive patients.

Changing the environmental conditions can also, therefore, lead to the elimination of undesirable behaviours. Behavioural therapies aim to do this through an analysis of the reinforcements (positive consequences) that are maintaining the behaviours at present. These will then be altered in the course of a therapy (there are a variety of these, such as behaviour modification, aversion, implosion or systematic desensitisation), and more appropriate behaviours will be encouraged. Targets will be set with the client, so the control is not totally in the hands of the therapist. For depression, the task of treatment is to increase the frequency of social behaviour and ensure that it is associated with pleasant outcomes.

Based on sound research, albeit mainly using animals, the behaviourist approach offers several useful therapies that have been shown to deal quickly and effectively with some mental disorders, such as phobias. However, it has been criticised for offering a 'quick fix' rather than getting to the root of the problem. It is also difficult to explain why, given the same environmental experiences, some people develop maladaptive behaviours whereas others do not, and others will develop different maladaptive behaviours.

The cognitive model

Cognitive psychologists such as Beck (1963) link abnormal behaviour with distorted thought patterns, which lead in turn to disordered behaviour. These distortions can include dichotomous thinking (seeing everything as either black or white) and overgeneralisation (e.g. assuming that because something has happened once, it will always happen). Depression, for example, may be associated with having a negative view of the self, the world and the future (known as the '**cognitive triad**' of depression). Such individuals maintain these biases by simply failing to notice any events that do not support their negative views. Other disorders may result from **social learning** processes, in which behaviour is observed in others and imitated (Bandura 1969).

Rather like the behaviourists, cognitive therapists are not concerned with the origins of these ways of thinking, so much as with changing them for more realistic and adaptive ones. Cognitive therapists aim to identify disordered thoughts and instigate programmes that will eliminate them, replacing them with more rational thought processes and behaviours. Therapies based on the cognitive model involve identifying and restructuring the problematic thought patterns. A depressive patient, for example, may be encouraged to keep a diary to identify the negative automatic thoughts that occur. These can then be challenged by logical argument and by practical tasks. Role play may also be used when it is felt that behaviours may be changed through observation and imitation.

Again the approach is a scientific one, based on theories that have been developed through research. Effective therapies have been devised to treat depression and panic disorder, for example, and more recently there is evidence that they can be used to control the hallucinations suffered by schizophrenics. However, just as the behaviourists consider that 'it could happen to anyone', there is the assumption that anyone could develop maladaptive thought processes, but the theorists fail to explain why only certain individuals seem to do so. In some cases, such as depression, the thought processes displayed are actually more realistic (they show greater accuracy when assessing risks, for example) than those of 'normal' individuals, so it is difficult to describe them as being 'maladaptive'.

The social constructionist model

This approach takes the view that there is no such thing as objectivity, and that our knowledge of ourselves and the world around us is simply based on social concensus; in other words, it is socially constructed. Because we cannot separate ourselves from our culture or our period in history, we cannot have an unbiased view of the world. This can be extended to mental disorder, making the point that what is perceived as abnormal (as already discussed) may vary, and that mental disorder itself may be socially created according to societal and clinical bias. Cultural and historical variation in the rate of occurrence of particular disorders may be attributed to this type of process, as we shall see in Chapters 3 and 4. Despite being a relatively recent approach, this has proved to be useful in understanding some of these variations.

The humanistic/existentialist model

The basic premise of this approach is that people are motivated towards personal growth and **self-actualisation** (realising their potential). They are free to make choices about their lives and accept responsibility for what they do. Mental disorder is thought to result when this is prevented; this may be associated with refusal to accept responsibility for actions, and with a negative view of the self (Rogers 1951). Depression in this instance could be the result of a blocking of this desire to self-actualise that we all share, or too great a mismatch between the individual's perceived self and the ideal self.

Therapies place an emphasis on understanding the conscious experiences of the individual, and objective scientific analysis is not considered appropriate. The best known of these, person-centred therapy, aims to provide conditions that will encourage personal growth by being non-directive and non-judgemental. Therapy aims to be holistic, and integrate various elements of behaviour so that the person becomes a unique being with the capacity to live 'authentically ' (i.e. be spontaneous, caring, open and realistic). These ideas have formed the basis of the very influential counselling movement, and have proved to be useful in dealing with the less severe disorders. Because they play down the role of the 'therapist-as-expert', they have been associated with the growth of community-based self-help groups in many spheres. Where clients are more severely disordered, and may not be very articulate, they have proved to be less useful. On the whole, these theorists have not carried out much scientific research in order to test their ideas.

The evolutionary approach

The emphasis here is on the adaptiveness of behaviour. The theory of evolution states that species have evolved through the process of natural selection. Because there is competition between individuals for limited resources, not all are able to survive. Those individuals who are well adapted to the environment will survive to pass on their genes (survival of the fittest) and those who are not well adapted will die out. The relevance here is that for mental disorder to persist in the population, it must be adaptive in some way. Depression, for example, may be adaptive when individuals are faced with situations in which it is impossible to win. Anxiety may have been adaptive when we were faced with 'fight or flight' confrontations, with dangerous animals for example. The fact that it is not adaptive nowadays illustrates **genome lag**, whereby genes that are no longer useful persist because insufficient time has passed for them to be eliminated.

This approach has encouraged us to look at the functions of behaviour. However, it clearly has no application to behaviours that are not genetically determined, and the applications to treatment (genetic engineering and counselling) are ethically dubious. It is also impossible to put these ideas to the test.

The family systems model

Instead of viewing the mentally disordered person as an individual, in this perspective the entire family is looked at as a social system. The idea is that mental disorder may not be located in the individual, but may be indicative of dysfunctional interaction patterns in the family as a whole (e.g. Bateson et al., 1956). Symptoms may develop as a way of distracting attention from areas of conflict. Anorexia nervosa, for example, has been attributed to families where members are over-involved with one another and overt conflict is avoided (Minuchin et al., 1978).

Family therapies based on such explanations focus on communication patterns in families, and use feedback to show family members what is happening. This can also be related to the shared beliefs and understandings of family members.

These therapies have proved useful with disturbed children, as well as with marital conflict and violence. The difficulty for theorists is that such patterns of interaction are very difficult to substantiate in scientific research, and much is therefore reliant on clinical judgement.

The socio-cultural model

This is the family systems approach on a larger scale, looking at cultural practices and social factors such as poverty for explanations of mental disorder. The variation in incidence of some disorders in different societies, or different groups within society (such as gender and social class), is used as the basis for arguments that social conditions can lead to psychopathology. Depression, for example, is more common in women, particularly those who live in adverse conditions with several young children. Hence it has been linked with isolation, lack of social support, lack of opportunity and feelings of powerlessness. Intervention would take the form of helping individuals to cope through, for example, building up their social support networks. Another possibility is to intervene at the level of the community or at the political level to bring about changes in social conditions.

The feminist model

This seeks to locate mental disorder (mainly in women) in the gender role allocated by society. The main focus has been on eating disorders. Anorexia, for example, has been linked with the powerlessness of women, and the need to strive to please, or to gain power, by focusing on their appearance. Fasting gives the satisfaction of being able to exert control over at least one aspect of life (Boskind-Lodahl & White 1978). A related view (Orbach 1978) is that self-denial is an integral part of the female role. Once this is accepted, and the woman ceases to recognise her own needs, anorexia may well follow. Change, in this model, can again focus on the individual or on society. Therapy with the individual can aim to free the woman from the constraints of the role provided by society. At the societal level, the aim is to bring about change in the gender roles themselves.

The eclectic approach

In practice, no single model can provide all the answers to mental disorder. Clinical psychologists are encouraged to take an eclectic approach, that is, to use all of the models, as appropriate. They may, for example, use a different model at different stages of treatment (Tyrer & Steinberg 1987) – a biological model initially, to bring the problem under control with drugs, followed by interventions based on behavioural and finally socio-cultural models. A biopsychosocial model represents a good integration of many of these ideas, and accommodates research evidence that all three types of factor may be involved in many disorders. One example of this approach is the diathesis–stress model, which implicates genetic vulnerability or other forms of long-term predisposition, together with environmental stress.

Working within one perspective can be seen to be very limiting, especially since, as implied earlier, mental disorders may be the result of causal chains. For example, the immediate cause may be stress, but this may only be problematic for individuals who have developed cognitive biases, which may in turn depend on abnormalities in brain chemistry. This makes it all the more important for treatment to be based on the **scientist-practitioner model**, which places emphasis on the uniqueness of each case. Careful consideration of each case during the assessment process should then lead to a choice of treatment that is tailored to the individual. The effectiveness of the chosen treatment can then be evaluated and alterations made as required on the basis of scientific analysis. However, clinicians may have preferences or specialisations which may dominate their view of the client and influence the course of treatment chosen, so it is important to be aware of the different viewpoints.

Progress exercise

Identify, in the form of a table, the main assumptions made by each of the aforementioned models about abnormal behaviour. The models can be divided into groups as follows:

Biomedical	Behaviourist	Psychodynamic	Cognitive

Social constructionist	Humanistic	Evolutionary

Family systems	Socio-cultural	Feminist

Make notes for each under the following headings (where possible):

* emphasis on past or present;
* basis of disorder;

- relevance of patient's thoughts;
- aim of therapy;
- who controls therapy;
- practical applications;
- limitations of model.

Chapter summary

In this chapter we have seen how the early conflict between seeing abnormal behaviour as demonic possession or as a medical illness continued to dominate thinking in this area until the Age of Reason around the beginning of the 19th century. The religious view was then replaced by a broader moral perspective. Subsequent institutional treatment varied from medical to moral, and has more recently been superseded by a community-based approach (although this still has a strong medical influence). The issue of defining abnormal behaviour has also been controversial, with legal definitions, several sets of psychological criteria and medical criteria having been considered. None of these appears to be totally satisfactory in covering all abnormal behaviours across cultures and eras. Issues and debates in psychology have been discussed in terms of their relationship to abnormal behaviour. Different psychological models of abnormality have also been described – biomedical, psychodynamic, behavioural, cognitive, social constructionist, humanistic, evolutionary, family systems, feminist and socio-cultural – and evaluated in terms of their assumptions and effectiveness. In the next chapter we shall explore the classification and assessment systems based on the medical model in more detail.

Read the following (real-life) cases and consider whether you would describe the individuals concerned as being mentally ill and in need of treatment. Assess each of them according to each of the different criteria for defining abnormality described earlier in the chapter.

Joyce B. lived on the street in a wealthy area of New York. She used the pavement as a toilet, soiled herself and smelt awful. Passers-by were

Review exercise

abused, and any money they gave her was burned. In 1987 she was picked up during a government campaign aimed at helping the homeless, taken to a psychiatric hospital and diagnosed as a paranoid schizophrenic. She protested that her civil rights had been violated. When lawyers from the Civil Liberties union had her reassessed, she was found not to be schizophrenic.

Darla S. refused to throw anything away. She hoarded rubbish to such an extent that she had to buy an ex-opera house to store it in. Among her possessions were theatrical costumes, a papier-mâché mermaid and stuffed alligators. She wore a fireman's coat and played in a kazoo band.

John S. had lived for 10 years in a cave that flooded with seawater at high tide. In the past he has walked from Land's End to John o' Groats in his bare feet, wearing only pyjamas. In order to raise money for conservation, he volunteered to spend 6 months in a cage at London Zoo as a human exhibit, but the authorities declined the offer.

Further reading

Carr, A. (2001) *Abnormal Psychology*. London: Routledge. (Useful comparison of family systems with other models of abnormality.)

Champion, L. & Power, M. (2000) *Adult Psychological Problems*. Hove, UK: Psychology Press. (Does an excellent job of relating the different models to a wide range of mental disorders, and is easy to read.)

Heller, T., et. al. (Eds) (1996) *Mental Health Matters*. London: Macmillan. (A selection of abridged articles on a range of mental health issues; each article is short and easy to read; several key writers included.)

Tyrer, P. & Steinberg, D. (1987) *Models for Mental Disorder*. London: Wiley. (Separate chapters on each model, plus an attempt to pull them all together; easy to read.)

2

Classification, assessment and diagnosis

- Background
- Diagnostic and Statistical Manual of Mental Disorders (DSM)
- Axes I and II: Major categories
- International Classification of Diseases (ICD)
- Clinical assessment procedures
- Evaluation of classification and diagnosis

Background

One of the key features of the scientific approach to any subject is that it is systematic. The subject matter is grouped into categories of items that share similar features, or subjected to some other form of logical organisation that makes it easier to see patterns or consistencies in what is observed. The natural sciences have long employed classification systems of various sorts, such as the periodic table of the elements used in chemistry or the phylogenetic systems of the biological sciences. In the 19th century, medical science began to make progress by identifying different illnesses and providing different forms of treatment for them. By comparison, there was very little consistency in the approach to abnormal behaviour. In Britain, a classification scheme was produced by the Statistical Committee of the Royal Medico-Psychological Association, but never utilised by the members. In Paris and America similar schemes also failed to gain acceptance.

One of these early schemes was that produced by Kraepelin (1883), who is often regarded as the founder of modern psychiatry. His system identified symptom groups or syndromes, which he considered to have organic causes, i.e. they were physically based. For example, severe mental illnesses were divided into dementia praecox (now known as schizophrenia), which was thought to result from a chemical imbalance, and manic-depressive psychosis, which was thought to result from metabolic irregularities. Kraepelin's system was the basis from which modern diagnostic schemes developed.

There are two major schemes in use at present. These are: the *Diagnostic and Statistical Manual of Mental Disorders* (DSM), originally produced by the American Psychiatric Association in 1952 and now in its fourth revision (1994); and the *International Classification of Diseases* (ICD) produced by the World Health Organisation in 1948 to cover both physical and mental illness, and now in its tenth version (1992, 1996). In both cases, the aim is to categorise mental disorder and thereby to provide diagnoses that can be linked with explanations and treatments. In the sections that follow we will examine these in more detail, with examples of cases that fit some of the categories. The procedures used to carry out the diagnosis, and an evaluation of the systems, will follow in the latter parts of the chapter.

Diagnostic and Statistical Manual of Mental Disorders (DSM)

DSM IV is a multi-axial system, that is, it suggests that each individual who presents with abnormal behaviour can be assessed on five different axes of functioning representing different aspects of the person's life. Axes I and II represent the clinical syndromes mentioned earlier. Axis III covers general medical conditions that may affect behaviour. Axis IV covers psychosocial and environmental problems, such as adverse life events. Axis V is a global assessment of psychological, social and occupational functioning. We will look at at each of these in turn, but note that only the first three are compulsory for diagnosis. Looking at all of them, however, in the course of a clinical assessment, should give a much better basis for treatment than simply providing an Axis I or Axis II diagnosis, as used to be the case. This is partly because the medical (Axis III) and social (Axis IV) problems that the individual has can also be given attention. It is also obvious that overall functioning (Axis V) may not always be closely linked with symptoms. Anxiety, for example, may or may not impair ability to work, depending on the nature of the person's job.

Axes I and II identify the major groups of clinical conditions; a list of these is provided in Tables 2.1 and 2.2, respectively. Axis I covers the major syndromes, and Axis II covers more chronic conditions that can either underlie them or occur separately. Most people would receive a diagnosis on one axis or the other, but it is possible to have both. Eating disorders and mental retardation, for example, can occur separately or together. Axis II is divided into two categories: personality disorders and mental retardation. Both are chronic problems that may underlie Axis I syndromes. Personality disorders are long term, rigid and maladaptive ways of behaving that cause stress and impair functioning. The types identified are listed in Table 2.2.

Mental retardation is associated with intellectual functioning that is below average by the age of 18 years, and associated deficits in functioning. It is divided into four groups. The most common form is mild retardation, which usually results from lack of early stimulation or inadequate early relationships. Moderate, severe and profound retardation are generally biological in origin. They include Down's syndrome (which results from a chromosomal abnormality), foetal alcohol syndrome (which results from maternal alcoholism), cretinism (the result of endocrine malfunction) and disorders due to brain damage or disease in childhood.

For each of the syndromes or conditions identified on the axes described, DSM gives details of diagnostic features, **prevalence** and diagnostic criteria. For some, there is also information about cultural differences, aetiology and treatment. In the next section, we will look at some of the major categories in more detail.

Axis III aims to draw the clinican's attention to the possible behavioural consequences of some medical conditions. An apparently psychological disorder may prove to have a medical cause and may respond better to medical treatment. For example (as noted earlier), hormone problems could result in mental retardation. Pregnancy complications or hormonal changes could lead to anxiety or a depressive disorder. In such cases, physical treatment may be more appropriate, and/or treatment may take a different form from that which would be given for anxiety or depression that has other origins. The conditions mentioned on Axis III include: infectious and parasitic diseases;

Table 2.1 DSM IV: the major clinical syndromes of Axis I

Schizophrenia and other psychotic disorders (marked by disturbances of thought, emotion, perception, loss of contact with reality, delusions and hallucinations)

Mood disorders (major depression, mania and bipolar disorder, i.e. swings between the two)

Anxiety disorders (excessive fears, phobias, obsessive-compulsive disorder, panic attacks, post-traumatic stress disorder and generalised anxiety)

Dissociative disorders (changes in normal consciousness such as loss of memory [amnesia] and identity [multiple personality disorder])

Psychoactive substance abuse disorders (problems related to the use of alcohol, nicotine or other psychoactive drugs)

Eating disorders (excessive concern about body weight and inability to regulate eating, as in self-starvation [anorexia] and alternate bingeing and purging [bulimia])

Somatoform disorders (excessive worry about health, and illness such as paralysis for which no physical cause can be found)

Factitious disorders (claims of illness leading to excessive help-seeking, as in Munchausen's syndrome)

Sexual and gender identity disorder (problems of identity, such as transsexualism, and of arousal, such as impotence, fetishism and voyeurism)

Sleep disorders (insomnia, apnea, narcolepsy and sleepwalking)

Delirium, dementia, amnestic and other cognitive disorders (resulting from ageing, poisoning or disease of the brain, such as Alzheimer's disease)

Disorders of infancy, childhood or adolescence (autism, attention deficit hyperactivity disorder or ADHD and learning disorders)

Impulse control disorders (pyromania or fire-setting, gambling, kleptomania)

Adjustment disorders (excessive anxiety and depression resulting from life stresses such as bereavement)

Table 2.2 DSM IV: personality disorders of Axis II

Antisocial personality (indifference to the feelings of others, criminal behaviour, lack of self-control and irresponsibility)

Obsessional personality (excessive adherence to rules and detail, striving for perfection, lack of emotional response)

Paranoid personality (tense, self-important, suspicious, sensitive to criticism)

Schizoid personality (solitary, withdrawn, poor social skills and limited emotional expression)

Histrionic personality (sociable, but egocentric, insincere and shallow, with emotional displays)

Narcissistic personality (self-important, attention-seeking, exhibitionistic, fantasises about success and power)

Dependent personality (lack self-esteem, cannot cope with everyday life, cannot assume responsibility)

endocrine, nutritional, metabolic and immune system disorders; diseases of the blood, circulatory, respiratory, digestive, nervous, genitourinary, skin and musculoskeletal systems; complications associated with pregnancy and the perinatal period, and injury and poisoning.

Axis IV is not compulsory, meaning that clinicians are not required to use this axis as part of their diagnostic process. However, it is useful because it draws attention to other aspects of functioning that may have contributed to the individual's problems, or may be the result of their behavioural difficulties. Either way, they may also need to be addressed in the course of treatment. The emphasis is on a holistic approach to treatment, an approach endorsed by the humanistic perspective mentioned in Chapter 1. In general, clinicians are encouraged to note only the problems that have arisen during the previous year, although there are cases (e.g. post-traumatic stress disorder) where a longer view may be necessary. The problems outlined for consideration are given in Table 2.3, together with examples.

Table 2.3 Axis IV of DSM: psychosocial and environmental problems

Type of problem	Examples
Primary support group	Death or ill-health of family member; sibling rivalry; sexual or physical abuse; divorce, remarriage or separation
Social environment	Lack of social support, loss of friendships, discrimination, retirement or other transition
Educational	Illiteracy, academic problems, conflict at school, bullying
Occupational	Stress, dissatisfaction or discord, unemployment or threats of redundancy
Housing	Homelessnesss, poor housing, discord with neighbours
Economic	Poverty, lack of welfare support
Health care	Inadequate services or insurance, lack of transport
Legal	Arrest or imprisonment, being a victim of crime or being involved in litigation

Axis V is the Global Assessment of Psychological, Social and Occupational Functioning (GAF scale). This provides a 100-point rating scale from 'superior functioning' down to 'unable to function' across all of the areas mentioned. Physical or environmental impairments are not included. A summary of the ratings is given in Table 2.4. There are also individual scales for measuring social and occupational functioning (SOFAS) and relationship functioning (GARF). As we have seen in Chapter 1, the legal criteria, as well as many of the DSM diagnostic criteria, may require these areas to be assessed. Some individuals with severe problems can nevertheless function well; others with comparatively mild problems may be completely unable to function.

Table 2.4 The Global Assessment of Functioning Scale from DSM IV	
Rating band	*Description of functioning*
100–91	Superior across a wide range of activities
90–81	Good in all areas, generally satisfied with life, minimal symptoms, only everyday problems
80–71	Transient symptoms in response to stress, only slight impairment in functioning
70–61	Mild symptoms (e.g. insomnia) or difficulties in functioning, but able to maintain personal relationships
60–51	Moderate symptoms (e.g. panic attacks) or difficulties in functioning (e.g. conflicts with others)
50–41	Serious symptoms of impairments (e.g. suicidal, unable to keep job)
40–31	Major impairment in several areas or impairment in communication
30–21	Serious impairment in communication (e.g. incoherent) or delusions, or inability to function in most areas (e.g. no job, home or friends)
20–11	Some danger of hurting self or others, or occasional failure to maintain personal hygiene, or extremely impaired communication (e.g. mute)
10–1	Danger of severely hurting self or others (suicidal or violent) or no personal hygiene

After using all of the scales to assess an individual, a clinician might come up with the following diagnosis:

Axis I: Generalised anxiety disorder
Axis II: Dependent personality disorder
Axis III: HIV positive
Axis IV: Problem related to occupation (lost job)
Axis V: GAF = 35

This is a relatively simple case; many individuals will have more than one identifiable problem – for example, there may be a somatoform disorder as well as an anxiety disorder.

Link each one of the behavioural problems on the left with one of the categories given on the right. Check your answers against Table 2.1 when you have finished.

Loss of contact with reality	Mood disorders
Excessive alcohol consumption	Impulse control disorders
Starving oneself	Schizophrenia and other psychotic disorders
Swinging between elation and depression	Anxiety disorders
Excessive fear some time after a traumatic experience	Psychoactive substance abuse disorders
Changing from one personality to another	Somatoform disorders
Gambling to excess	Dissociative disorders
A physical problem with no physical cause	Eating disorders

Axes I and II: major categories

In this section, we will be taking a closer look at the DSM IV diagnostic criteria for just five of the conditions listed in Axes I and II. These categories are based on the presence of clusters of symptoms, an approach endorsed by the medical model described in Chapter 1. Note that other models (e.g. the humanistic approach) may not accept this way of dealing with mental disorder. The conditions that we will be looking at here are: schizophrenia; major depression; obsessive-compulsive disorder; bulimia nervosa; antisocial personality. Space limitations preclude any more coverage than this, but the interested reader is referred to more detailed texts at the end of this chapter, and to the text in this series on psychopathology. A case study is also provided for each condition by way of illustration.

Schizophrenia

CASE STUDY 2.1 Schizophrenia (Lavender 2000)

John was referred to a psychiatrist at the age of 22, after leaving home to go to college. Prior to that, he lived at home with his mother and sister, and had always had problems making friends. Living in a shared house with other students proved to be difficult, and he spent increasing amounts of time in his room. He began to think that the other people in the house were plotting against him, and imagined that they were standing outside his door and shouting abuse. As his work began to suffer, he began to have paranoid thoughts about his college lecturers. This eventually extended to the belief that MI5 had bugged the house with microphones hidden in the walls. After he left college and returned to the family home, he had little energy and no interests. He remained unemployed and continued to avoid contact with anyone outside the home.

This is an example of a psychotic disorder, a group of conditions that share the feature of being divorced from reality and lacking any insight into the condition. The symptoms vary widely, and hence DSM gives details of five subtypes – catatonic, paranoid, disorganised, undifferentiated and residual. Here we will just be looking at the general picture. Broadly speaking, there are two groups of symptoms

– the positive symptoms, which consist of excessive behaviours, and the negative symptoms, which consist of behavioural deficits. The behaviours affected may be cognitive, emotional and psychomotor.

Positive symptoms include thought disturbances such as delusions. These are thoughts that appear to most people to be misinterpretations of reality, for example, delusions of persecution or of grandeur, or a conviction that thoughts are being inserted into the mind by aliens. Thoughts, and their expression in language, are frequently confused, leading to loose associations (shifting from one topic to another), and perseveration (repetition of statements). Hallucinations (perceptions that occur in the absence of the appropriate external stimuli), particularly the hearing of voices, may occur. Movements may be excessive in style or amount. Emotions are often inappropriate to the occasion, such as laughing at bad news.

Negative cognitive symptoms may include a tendency to say very little (alogia). Emotionally, the person may report an inability to feel pleasure (anhedonia), display very little emotion (blunted or flat affect), or show inappropriate emotional responses. There may be social withdrawal, and loss of volition leading to apathy. Movement may become repetitive, or there may be no movement at all, a state known as catatonia.

The diagnostic criteria for schizophrenia are shown in Table 2.5. Signs of the disorder must persist for at least 6 months (unlike

Table 2.5 Diagnostic criteria for schizophrenia

The criteria have been identified as involving the presence of two or more of the following characteristic symptoms for a significant proportion of the time during a 1-month period:

delusions;

hallucinations;

disorganised (e.g. incoherent) speech;

grossly disorganised or catatonic behaviour;

negative symptoms such as lack of emotion, speech or motivation.

ICD 10 criteria). This must be associated with marked inability to function in at least one major area, such as work, relationships and self-care. Signs of disturbance must continue for at least 6 months, and must not be due to mood disorder, schizoaffective disorder, substance abuse or medical conditions. There are also four subtypes: paranoid (delusions and hallucinations predominate); catatonic (motor disturbance predominates); disorganised (emotional disorder and disorganisation of speech and thought predominate); and undifferentiated (apathy, loss of interest and social withdrawal).

Major depression

CASE STUDY 2.2 Major depression (Clipson & Steer 1998)

Jennifer was persuaded by a priest (whom she had gone to see about her relationship difficulties) that she needed to see a counsellor. She had experienced problems with relationships, including parental, since childhood. She had never known her father, felt distant from her stepfather, and had a mother who used alcohol to alleviate her own relationship problems. After an initial abusive relationship, she had found herself a more suitable partner. All seemed to be well until he began to pay less attention to her and became more absorbed in his job. At the same time, she had lost her job, and showed little inclination to find another. She started to become less interested in her old activities, and neglected her friends. She felt useless, and often stayed in bed all day crying, particularly when her partner was away on business, which increased her feelings of being unable to cope. Despite being presented with evidence to the contrary, she felt that his friends and family disliked her. Finally, she began to think about committing suicide.

This is one of a group of disorders characterised mainly by emotional disturbance. Other areas of functioning that may be affected include cognitive, motivational, behavioural and physical. The mood changes are severe and long-lasting, and include feelings of intense sadness and emptiness, and loss of pleasurable feelings such as affection and enjoyment. Cognitively, patients have a very negative view of life, present and future, and of themselves. They may feel so worthless that they think they would be better off dead. There may be confusion and memory impairment. Their motivation to carry out everyday activities is considerably reduced, and to do anything is a great effort. Activity levels are low, movements slow, and they may stay in bed all day. There are also physical symptoms such as loss of appetite, constipation, loss of sexual drive, intolerance of noise and bright lights, and weight changes.

The diagnostic criteria for major depression are shown in Table 2.6. These symptoms should cause significant impairment in key areas of functioning, and should not be attributable to substance abuse, medical conditions or bereavement within the last 2 months.

Table 2.6 Diagnostic criteria for major depression
Five or more of the following (including at least one of the first two) must be present most of the time during the same 2-week period:
depressed mood;
loss of interest or pleasure in most activities;
changes in weight or appetite;
reduced or increased sleep;
restlessness or lethargy;
feelings of worthlessness or guilt;
inability to concentrate or make decisions;
recurrent thoughts of death and suicide.

Obsessive-compulsive disorder

CASE STUDY 2.3 Obsessive-compulsive disorder (Clipson & Steer 1998)

Phillip's father was the manager of a health food shop. Even as a child, Phillip was very tidy, unlike his brother. As he grew up, he became more particular about cleanliness and tidiness issues. His college work was always very neatly done, and he washed his hands several times each day. He was particularly upset by having to share a toilet seat with flat-mates when he went to college. Several relationships with women had ended due to his hoarding and obsessive behaviours. Every morning, he had to carry out several rituals in the bathroom, which necessitated him getting up at 4.30 am. His shaving equipment was laid out precisely, all items facing the right direction and in the correct order and position, and he shaved according to an exact pattern. Any error or interruption meant that he had to repeat the process from the beginning. When driving to work, if he travelled over a bump in the road, he would have to go back and make sure that he had not hit anybody. The journey would generally take twice as long as it should have, and he would be late for work. As a result, he had already lost one job and was having difficulties with the current one.

This is an example of the group of conditions known as the anxiety disorders. The characteristic feature of the group is, as the name implies, fear and anxiety that appear to be groundless. Although anxiety may be observed in some other disorders, such as schizophrenia, in this case the individual is aware that the behaviour is unreasonable but simply cannot control it; such insight is not found in the more severe conditions. Obsessions are recurrent thoughts, images or impulses that invade consciousness and are very difficult to control. They may take the form of doubts (e.g. about whether the door was locked when the person left the house), fears about doing things that are prohibited (e.g. dancing on a gravestone), persistent images (e.g. of a baby being flushed down a toilet), impulses (e.g. to drink a pot of ink), or thoughts about the future. Compulsions are repetitive, stereotyped behaviours that have to be performed, often in response to the obsessive thoughts, in order to keep anxiety at bay. They usually take the form of counting (e.g. paving stones on the way to work), cleaning (e.g. wiping door handles after every use), checking (e.g. that doors and windows are locked several times before leaving home) or avoidance (e.g. refusing to touch any other member of the family).

The diagnostic criteria for obsessive-compulsive disorder are shown in Table 2.7. These must interfere significantly with normal functioning, must take up more than 1 hour per day and must be distressing. They must not be due to another Axis I disorder or to substance abuse or medical conditions.

Table 2.7 Diagnostic criteria for obsessive-compulsive disorder
Obsessions or compulsions must be present, and the individual must be aware that they are unreasonable. Obsessions are defined by:
recurrent, intrusive thoughts, impulses or images that cause anxiety;
these must extend beyond everyday worries;
the individual must recognise that they are produced by his/her own mind and must try to suppress or neutralise them.
Compulsions are defined by:
repetitive behaviours that the person feels compelled to carry out;
they are carried out with the aim of reducing distress but are excessive or not logically related to the problem concerned.

Bulimia nervosa

CASE STUDY 2.4 Bulimia nervosa (Clipson & Steer 1998)

A child of two successful parents, Dana was persuaded to see a psychologist when her boyfriend found her vomiting after a bingeing session. Her father was a lawyer, obsessed with success, and her mother was a very attractive woman who was obsessed with appearances. Dana had never felt able to satisfy either of them. Weight control had always been an issue since she was teased about it as a child, and she had learnt about controlling it by vomiting from a friend. She had also seen a psychiatrist for depression in the past, and regularly abused several drugs including alcohol. By the age of 22, she had reached the stage where she was bingeing and purging several times a day, and often had to shoplift the food needed as she could not afford to buy it. She believed that she was overweight, although she was not, had not had a period for several years and had no interest in sex.

This is part of a group of eating disorders. It usually occurs in females, after a period of intense dieting, and involves episodes of uncontrolled overeating (binges) followed by purges (e.g. self-induced vomiting, use of laxatives or diuretics, excessive exercise or fasting) by way of compensation. Weight usually stays within the normal range, although it may fluctuate noticeably. The binges may be triggered by tension or depression, possibly as the result of some upsetting event. Typically, there will be about 10 episodes in a week. Massive amounts of high-calorie, 'forbidden' foods will be gobbled down in secret without even tasting them; this will be followed by feelings of guilt and depression, together with fears about weight gain.

Bulimics often have a history of mood swings and low tolerance for frustration and boredom. They find it difficult to control their impulses, are generally quite emotional, and may also abuse alcohol and other drugs. The physical consequences of bulimia are considerable in severe cases: tooth decay may result from the acidic content of vomit; potassium deficiency may result in heart or intestinal problems; acute dilation or rupture of the stomach is possible; and callouses may develop on the back of the hand where it rubs against the teeth when inducing vomiting. There are also social consequences, since social activities may be restricted as a result of the amount of time and money devoted to bingeing and purging. The diagnostic criteria for bulimia nervosa are given in Table 2.8.

Table 2.8 Diagnostic criteria for bulimia nervosa
Recurrent episodes of binge eating, which is identifiable as eating more food than most people would over a specific period of time, with a feeling of lack of control over the eating.
Recurrent compensatory behaviour (e.g. vomiting, laxative use, fasting, exercising to excess) to prevent weight gain (subtypes of purging and non-purging are identified by the nature of the compensatory behaviours).
Bingeing and compensating should occur at least twice weekly for 3 months.
Self-evaluation is overly influenced by body shape/weight
These behaviours do not occur solely during anorexic episodes.

Antisocial personality disorder

CASE STUDY 2.5 Antisocial personality disorder (Clipson & Steer 1998)

Following the divorce of their parents, Kurt and his brother both suffered physical abuse at the hands of their father before being returned to the custody of the mother. She was a heavy user of drugs and alcohol. Problems at school led to him being expelled, and eventually being categorised as severely emotionally disturbed. At the age of 12, he was caught shoplifting. By 14 he was committing burglaries. After running away from home, he lived by theft and drug-dealing, and was eventually put into a home for juvenile offenders until he was 18. On his release, drug-dealing became his main source of income, and he continued to be arrested for minor offences. Relationships with females were short-lived. He came to the attention of the authorities again when, after several episodes of domestic violence, he stabbed his current girlfriend and was convicted of attempted murder. He was hostile to the psychologist and refused to answer any of the questions put to him. The psychologist found that he had little tolerance for stress and felt inadequate. He had come to deal with all his problems by using drugs and violence, neither of which he could control. His own satisfaction was his sole motivation, and he had little regard for the feelings of others.

This is one of a group of personality disorders in which the behaviour problem impairs social or occupational functioning. The antisocial personality is also referred to as sociopathic or psychopathic. The main characteristic is that they cause a great deal of distress to others, rather than feeling distressed themselves. Repeated criminal behaviour is likely, although not all criminals have an antisocial personality, nor are all antisocial personality cases criminals. Offences often include violence, prostitution, theft, drugs- or alcohol-related offences. Behaviour is irresponsible in a variety of ways. For example: regular employment is unlikely; there may be little or no evidence of parental behaviour; relationships may be limited to short-term sexual liaisons; lying and impulsivity may be evident, and may lead to financial problems; there may be little evidence of any feelings of guilt or remorse. The diagnostic criteria are given in Table 2.9.

Table 2.9 Diagnostic criteria for antisocial personality disorder

The individual should be at least 18 years old, with previous history of conduct disorder before the age of 15.

Since 15, there should be evidence of disregard for the rights of others, as shown by at least three of the following: repeated unlawful acts; deceitfulness; impulsivity; physical aggression; disregard for the safety of self or others; irresponsible behaviour; lack of remorse.

This should not be part of a schizophrenic or manic disorder.

Consider each of the five case studies presented in the chapter in the light of the five DSM axes, and present as full a diagnosis as you can. Note for each of them which Axis I and II criteria their symptoms may fulfil, and whether any Axis III and IV problems may be present. Then suggest a rating for Axis V.

Progress exercise

International Classification of Diseases (ICD)

ICD 10 has a section devoted to mental disorders; the main categories are given in Table 2.10. There is also a multiaxial system for mental disorders that affect children and adolescents. According to this, Axis

Table 2.10 ICD 10: major categories of mental disorder	
Category	*Examples*
Organic disorders	Alzheimer's and amnesia due to organic damage/disease
Schizophrenia, schizotypal and delusional disorders	Schizophrenia
Psychoactive substance use disorders	Alcohol and drug-related problems
Mood (affective) disorders	Depression, mania and manic depression
Neurotic, stress-related and somatoform disorders	Phobias, generalised anxiety, obsessive-compulsive disorder, multiple personality
Behavioural disorders associated with physiological and physical factors	Eating disorders, sexual dysfunction not organically caused
Disorders of adult personality and behaviour	Personality disorder, habit and impulse disorder, disorders of gender, identity and sexual preference
Mental retardation	Mild, severe and profound
Disorders of psychological development	Disorders of speech, language and learning, autism, Asperger's syndrome
Disorders with onset in childhood and adolescence	Attentional and conduct disorders, tics, enuresis, stuttering
Unspecified	

II is specific delays in development, Axis III is intellectual level, Axis IV is medical conditions, Axis IV is abnormal psychosocial conditions and Axis VI is the global assessment of functioning.

Comparing DSM and ICD

As both ICD and DSM are classifying the same behaviours, it should not be too surprising that they are very similar. Both, for example, have a category for psychoactive substance-related disorders, for mental retardation and for personality disorders. However, there are some differences worth pointing out here. The most obvious difference is that (adult) ICD has only one axis, whereas DSM has five. ICD also appears to have fewer categories; for example, ICD groups neurotic, stress-related and somatoform disorders into one group, whereas DSM has four groups (anxiety, dissociative, adjustment and somatoform disorders) covering the same behaviours. Similarly, ICD has one group for disorders of adult personality and behaviour, whereas DSM has four (personality disorder, sexual and gender identity disorders, impulse control disorders and factitious disorders). On the other hand, DSM has one group for disorders first diagnosed in infancy, childhood or adolescence, whereas ICD has two (behavioural and emotional disorders with onset usually occurring in childhood or adolescence, and disorders of psychological development).

Using Tables 2.1, 2.2, and 2.10, draw up a parallel chart to display the DSM and ICD categories alongside one another, to show the similarities and differences.

Progress exercise

Clinical assessment procedures

Following referral, assessment by clinicians will be the first step in the process of helping persons suffering from mental disorder. It will take different forms depending on the training and biases of the clinician (for example, a counsellor assesses but does not diagnose) but the basic principles will remain the same. In this section we will look at the general principles and then the range of methods that may be used.

Principles of assessment

What is clinical assessment and why is it used?

Clinical assessment is the process of gathering information about a client in order to gain a better understanding of the person (Kendall & Norton-Ford 1982). An assessment method (or methods) will be chosen by the clinician, and the results interpreted and written up in a report. Assessment will be carried out for three main reasons (although not all assessments will involve all three):

- *Diagnosis and screening* Diagnosis is the process of outlining the symptoms of the patient and seeing how they fit the syndromes detailed in the classification system. To identify the client's problem is an important first step in deciding on the correct treatment. Diagnosis may also be required in order to determine whether or not the client is to be judged sane for legal purposes. Screening may be needed to select clients who would be most appropriate for particular treatment programmes.
- *Evaluation of therapeutic interventions* It is important to measure the behaviours that are being targeted before the intervention begins, in order to have a baseline against which post-intervention measures can be compared.
- *Research* Quantitative or qualitative measurement is essential to any programme that is attempting to test hypotheses about the causes of behaviour problems, such as the link between media violence and aggression in children for example.

What are the properties of a good assessment system?

As has already been made clear, assessment needs to provide a measurement of the behaviours concerned. This may be qualitative (simply indicating what type of behaviours are displayed), or quantitative measurement (indicating how much of the behaviour is shown). The latter is usually preferred because it is more precise. In order to be considered scientific, the measurement must also be objective; this means that it should not be influenced by anything other than the behaviour under consideration. In particular, it is important to rule out the influence that the clinician may have at all stages of the assessment process. As indicated in Chapter 1, it is also necessary in some cases to compare the person being assessed with the population at large in order to see if they are abnormal. In order to do this, the test or procedure used must provide some idea of population norms for that behaviour. The procedure by which this is done is referred to as standardisation, and involves giving the test to a large sample of the population in order to find the average score.

The key issues to consider when evaluating an assessment system are reliability and validity. By implication, these issues also relate to the classification system (i.e. DSM or ICD) that is used in conjuction with assessment, since they cannot be evaluated independently. We will be returning to reliability and validity throughout the chapter, so it is important to explain their meaning at this stage. You need to bear them in mind as we explore the assessment techniques.

Reliability

A reliable test is one on which an individual will achieve the same score each time he or she is tested. This means that it must be stable across time (**test–retest reliability**) – assuming of course that the behaviour concerned is stable. Anxiety, for example, may be expected to fluctuate, whereas compulsive behaviours should be stable. It must also yield the same results irrespective of who administers the test (known as interscorer or **interrater reliability**); this requires the scoring system to be clear-cut, so that it cannot be interpreted differently by different users. Finally, it must show internal consistency, in that all of the test items must be good indicators of the behaviour concerned (measured by Cronbach's alpha or **split-half reliability**). If some are not, they may erroneously inflate scores on the test.

Validity

Validity refers to whether or not the test actually measures what it claims to measure. A personality test may be reliable, in the sense of being consistent, for example, but it may be a test of intelligence or literacy rather than personality if the questions are too difficult to understand. It follows that a test may be valid for one purpose, but not for another. A PET scan, for example, is a valid measure of brain activity but not of intelligence. There are several different types of validity. **Face validity** refers to whether the items in the test seem to be good examples of the behaviour concerned. If we are considering aggression, for example, is it appropriate to include items about verbal as well as physical aggression? **Construct validity** requires the test to be based on a theory for which there is some support. Many tests of personality, for example, are based on particular theories; the same is not true of tests of intelligence, where the tests often preceded the theories and the theories are general rather than specific. Validity can also be shown by the test being correlated with another measure of the same thing (sometimes called **criterion validity**). If this is carried out at the same time, this is known as **concurrent validity**. A PET scan, for example, can be used as an indicator of Alzheimer's disease, against which other assessment procedures can be validated. If the other measure is given later, it is called **predictive validity**; thus an intelligence test score may be related to future academic progress.

Both reliability and validity will be affected by the applicability of the test used to the people it is used with (in terms of factors such as culture and age, for example), and by other biases such as responses to any emotional content in the test, complexity of questions and general response biases. We will consider these more fully in the next section.

In practical situations, it is also necessary to consider the test's **clinical utility**. This can be described as its 'hit rate' – how often it identifies correctly that someone has a particular problem or is clear of it. A good test should lead to a high proportion of correct diagnoses and should do this more quickly and cheaply than other methods. A weak test may incorrectly miss people with problems (false negatives) or give positive diagnoses to those who do not have problems (false positives), both of which can be harmful. Cost-effectiveness assessments have to bear this in mind. A particularly good example is given by the case of child abuse, where mistakes can have grave consequences. Errors are particularly likely if the condition concerned is rare, i.e. it has a low base rate. (Meehl & Rosen 1955).

Define the meaning of the following:

test–retest reliability; interrater reliability; split-half reliability; face validity; construct validity; concurrent validity; predictive validity.

When you have finished you can check your answers against the terms given in the glossary.

Methods of assessment

A variety of methods are available to clinicians, all of which have advantages and disadvantages. All measurement is subject to errors, so we need to know the tolerance limits of each method and the best circumstances in which to apply it. Some methods are more suitable for certain aspects of functioning, therefore to obtain an overall picture a combination will be used on any particular case. The assessment needs to cover the case history (often known as the core assessment), behaviour, social and cognitive functioning, personality and mood, and neuropsychological functioning, although not all of these will be required in every case.

Clinical interviews

Talking to the client is often the first stage of the assessment process. As well as gathering information about the presenting problem, including current feelings and concerns, relationships, employment and family issues, and personal history, the interview can tell the clinician a great deal in an indirect manner by providing an opportunity to observe the way that the client interacts. Posture, gestures, facial expressions, eye contact etc., can all provide useful information. Encouraging openness and free communication is essential if the interview is to be useful, so establishing rapport with the client and giving assurances of confidentiality are crucial at the outset. Computers have been introduced by some clinicians to conduct initial interviews. This obviously saves money and the clinician's time, but in turn reduces the opportunities for gathering information about nonverbal communication. In the medical sphere, it has been found that people will sometimes reveal more to a computer than to a doctor (presumably because they are less embarrassed), so computers may have advantages with some clients.

Clinicians from different persuasions will focus on different areas during the interview: for example, psychodynamic theorists may be more concerned with childhood experiences than behaviourists would be; socio-cultural theorists may be more interested in social conditions.

There are many different types of interview. One important distinction is between unstructured and structured interviews. In a structured interview, the client is asked open-ended questions and allowed to discuss whatever she or he feels is important. This has the advantage that the client, rather than the clinician, can determine the direction that the conversation takes. In the latter, the clinician uses a prepared list of questions (e.g. the Diagnostic Interview Schedule or DIS, devised by Robins et al. 1981), which has the advantage of allowing comparisons to be made between the responses of different individuals. It also ensures that no important issues or aspects of behaviour are omitted. Panic disorder, for example, may be explored by initially asking a screening question ('Have you ever felt anxious in a situation where most people would not feel afraid?'), followed by precise questions to assess severity ('Did you sweat?'). There are also versions for children, e.g. the DIS-C (Costello et al. 1985). The model that the clinician subscribes to may well dictate preference for one type of interview over another – a psychodynamic or a humanistic theorist may prefer an unstructured interview, for example, and behavioural, cognitive and medical theorists may prefer structured interviews.

A **mental state** interview may also be used, which aims to evaluate the current functioning of the client. It is presented in a structured form to ensure that particular areas are covered. Appearance, general behaviour, speech, mood, thought content, abnormal beliefs and experiences, memory, attention, values, and awareness of where they are and what is going on around them (orientation in time and space) will all be assessed.

Interviews provide most of the information required for the core assessment (case history), although some may come from the referral letter and from other parties such as social workers or relatives. Lindsay and Powell (1994) suggest that this should cover all of the items listed in Table 2.11.

Table 2.11 Information needed for the core assessment
Reason for referral, including client's description of problem(s) and immediate reason for seeking help
History of difficulties
Medical, occupational, educational, sexual and marital history
Current situation (job/home) and difficulties resulting from problem
Effect of problem on biological functioning
Effect of problem on others
Abnormal moods, thoughts, sensory experiences
Current appearance, behaviour and cognitive functioning
Attitude towards problem
Current drug use
Family history of psychological problems

Interviews also contribute to the functional analysis of behaviour, (which identifies the reinforcements maintaining behaviour), and to the assessment of social functioning at work, at home, in relationships and in leisure activities.

EVALUATION

Interviews are obviously the major source for a lot of useful information, but their reliability and validity are both questionable. The client may not be totally honest, may be embarrassed, or may simply make errors when recalling past events. The very nature of some syndromes, such as depression, where self-esteem is affected, means that clients are unlikely to recall personal experiences accurately. The clinician may be biased, or may affect the client's behaviour in a variety of ways, and the client may also affect the clinician. Paurohit et al. (1982), for example, have shown that the race, sex, age and appearance of the interviewer may influence the client's responses. Clinicians may also vary in their interpretation of information, and they may make errors when recording what was said, especially if they do not make detailed notes at the time. First impressions may affect the way that subsequent information is interpreted (Luchins 1957). Even when the same questions are asked of the same clients, it has been shown that different clinicians will obtain different information and form different conclusions (Langwieler & Linden 1993). Clinical bias will be discussed again in the final section of this chapter, and is also an important theme of Chapters 3 and 4.

Observations

In some cases it is desirable to see behaviours as they occur, rather than discuss them in an interview. The clinical observation allows this to be done, either in the natural setting or in a controlled environment. The interaction of a child with other family members, for example, may be recorded in the home, or in a mock living room in the clinic using a one-way mirror. Barkley (1981) used this approach with hyperactive children and their mothers. If the observation is to take place in the home, a participant observer may be employed; this is the use of someone with whom the child is familiar to carry out the observation. Teachers, for example, can be asked to give ratings of behaviour in the classroom using the Conners' Teacher Rating Scale (1969). The advantage of this is that the child may behave more naturally. Typically, a relatively small number of behaviours (known as 'target behaviours') will be selected for observation, for reasons of practicality. Their frequency of occurrence and/or severity will be recorded over a specified period of time, as in the example in Table 2.12. Standardised scales, such as the Family Interaction Coding Scale (Patterson et al. 1982), may be used for recording purposes.

It is important to look at not only the frequency of occurrence but at the sequences and patterns of behaviours to see what immediately causes them. This is the key feature of **functional analysis**, carried out by behavioural psychologists, to identify the reinforcements maintaining the client's undesirable behaviours. This can be carried out using the STAR system as a guide, and involves identifying:

Table 2.12 Behavioural checklist for performance anxiety (after Paul 1966)

Behaviour	Time period (minutes)								
	1	2	3	4	5	6	7	8	9
Face pale									
Muscles tense									
Swallows									
Voice shakes									
Stammers									
Lack of eye contact									

S: the setting conditions or environments in which the behaviour occurs;

T: the triggers or specific events that prompt the behaviour;

A: the antecedent events that occur before the behaviour;

R: the results of the behaviour for the client.

In some cases, where behaviours are infrequent, where the clinician cannot spend a long time with the client, or where thought processes (which cannot be monitored by outside observers) are involved, clients may be asked to **self-monitor**. For example, bulimics may be asked to record the feelings and situations that lead to the urge to binge, or obsessionals to record the frequency of their obsessive thoughts. This is useful to establish the antecedents that trigger behaviours.

Another type of observation occurs when measures are taken of physiological and neurological behaviours. Physiological measures such as changes in heart rate, blood pressure or muscle tension can be used to indicate the level of a client's anxiety. A plethysmograph can be used to record blood flow in the vagina or penis, as a measure of sexual arousal when assessing sexual disorders. In the case of neuro-logical behaviours, instruments such as the electro-encephalogram or a scanner such as **PET** (Positron Emission Tomograph) can be used to record the electrical activity of the brain. The aim is to detect the presence and extent of brain damage or malfunction. Baxter et al. (1987), for example, measured the brain activity of obsessive-compulsive patients during various activities, compared with that of controls. They found that the patients showed greater activity in the caudate nuclei than did the controls. Andreasen et al. (1990) used scanners to explore the size of the ventricles (fluid-filled spaces) in the brains of schizophrenics, compared to those of normal controls. The research showed that the ventricles were larger in the schizophrenics, particularly on the left side of the brain.

EVALUATION.

The observational method is particularly useful with children or other clients (such as schizophrenics) who are unwilling or unable to co-operate with interviews or tests. Some researchers (e.g. Barlow 1977) have found observations to be better indicators of recovery after treatment than interviews and tests (see Figure 2.1). However, observation is restricted in its application, since only observable, frequent behaviours can be studied; maladaptive thought processes cannot.

It is also limited in reliability and validity. The most important reliability issue is that of inter-observer reliability – do different

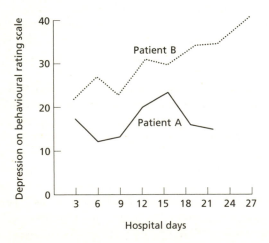

Figure 2.1 **Observation of depressive behaviours**

observers give the same results? What one observer interprets as aggression, for example, another may not. It is generally found that initially they may not agree (Banister et al. 1994), although careful training and the use of checklists and clear definitions of the behaviours can improve this (Goodwin 1995). Self-monitoring may have particular problems with respect to reliability. It can be improved by motivating clients using rewards, by training, and by informing them that their monitoring is being checked (Nelson et al. 1975). **Reactivity** is the term used to describe change in behaviour that can result from observation (particularly self-observation). It is generally found that 'good' behaviour increases, and 'bad' behaviour decreases, indicating a therapeutic effect.

Validity may be limited by the change in behaviour of the client when he or she is aware of being watched – the audience effect – and also by the situation chosen for the observation (ecological validity). A child may misbehave at home, for example, but not at school (Simpson & Halpin 1986). Zeigob et al. (1975) showed that when mothers knew that they were being observed, they behaved more positively towards their children.

Physiological and neurophysiological observations are also subject to difficulties, although they are very precise when used properly. The equipment required is expensive and not always readily available. A great deal of training is usually required before it can be used with any accuracy. It often requires that recordings are taken in the artificial environment of the laboratory, and only limited behaviours can be carried out at the same time. The equipment itself may be frightening, and may change behaviour. It is not always easy to link any observed changes with the client's emotional state; for example, blood pressure may change as a result of many factors and feelings and not simply as a result of anxiety.

Psychometric tests

Psychometric tests are specially devised instruments (often paper and pencil tests) that take a small sample of the client's behaviour in order to make inferences about broader aspects of their functioning. There are many different types for different purposes. For example, the Halstead-Reitan test battery (Reitan & Davison 1974) and Bender-Gestalt test (Bender 1938) have been devised to assess different areas of neurological functioning. The Significant Others Scale (SOS) devised by Power et al. (1988) provides ratings of how much social support clients expect from others in different situations. There are also specific tests for screening clients for psychiatric distress, such as the General Health Questionnaire or GHQ (Goldberg & Williams 1988). Long-term difficulties can be assessed using the Symptom Check-List-90-Revised (SCL-90-R), devised by Derogatis in 1977. This consists of 90 questions designed to measure nine dimensions of psychopathology, including obsessive-compulsive problems, depression, paranoia, phobia, anxiety etc. Here we will look at intelligence and aptitude tests, personality questionnaires and projective tests.

Intelligence tests aim to provide a measure of general cognitive ability, often in the form of an intelligence quotient (IQ). There are many different tests available. Some, such as the Stanford-Binet and the Wechsler Adult Intelligence Scale (WAIS), are administered to individuals, and these are more likely to be used as clinical instruments. The WAIS has 11 subtests, including digit span, block design and vocabulary tests. There are other Wechsler tests for preschool children (the WPPSI) and for older children (the WISC). Other intelligence tests, such as the AH series (AH2, AH3 etc) are designed to be administered to people in a group situation. Many of the tests, but not all, are timed. Aptitude tests, such as the British Ability Scales, are similar but more specific, in that they focus on one particular ability, such as mechanical or spatial for example. Performance can then be compared with that of others of the same age. Many clinicians prefer a rapid, nonverbal screening test such as Raven's Progressive Matrices.

EVALUATION.

Most of the tests in current use have been carefully constructed and standardised on large samples of the population. They have high reliability in that the results obtained by the same person on different occasions will be similar (Kline 1993), and high internal consistency. Test administrators, however, must always be on guard for illness and motivational and emotional problems that may affect a particular client's performance on the test. They also show good concurrent validity, relating well to school performance for example (Neisser et al. 1996). However, their predictive validity is not always as good, probably because performance on either the test or the other measure can be affected by factors such as motivation. Construct validity can also be debated, as there is no agreed theory about what intelligence is. In connection with this, some psychologists (e.g. Gardner 1983; Sternberg 1985) have argued that the intelligence tests in current use focus on only a narrow spectrum of skills, ignoring 'streetwise intelligence' and interpersonal intelligence, for example. Finally, intelligence tests have been criticised for not being culture-fair, in the sense that individuals from minority groups or deprived backgrounds may be less familiar with the types of language or items used in the test, and may therefore not perform as well as other groups. Since the tests play an important role in the assessment of mental retardation and brain damage, as well as in the educational and occupational spheres, it is important to recognise this.

Personality questionnaires (or inventories) are self-report scales that require the client to respond to a series of statements by indicating whether or not each one applies to them. There are many different tests, all aimed at measuring different aspects of personality. Other tests measure affect or emotion (such as the Beck Depression Inventory), cognition or social skills. The Beck scale, for example, consists of 21 items with four responses to each, such as: I can work as well as I used to; it takes extra effort to get started doing something; I have to push myself to do anything; I can't work at all. One of the best known inventories is the Minnesota Multiphasic Personality Inventory (Hathaway & McKinley 1943). The current version (produced in 1989) contains 567 items such as 'I go to a party every week', 'I often feel hopeless about the future' and 'I am easily embarrassed' (each scored 'true', 'false' or 'cannot say'). It provides an assessment on 10 basic clinical scales as well as functioning at work, tendency to abuse drugs and vulnerability to eating disorders. The scales include schizophrenia, paranoia, depression, mania, introversion, hypochondria, hysteria, and fears and obsessions. On each scale, scores can range from 0–120. The normal score is 50 and a score above 70 is considered indicative of deviance. There are also scales that aim to detect lying, careless or defensive responding, or response sets such as a tendency to give negative answers. Tests such as the MMPI can be used together with more specific tests such as the State–Trait Anxiety Inventory (Spielberger 1983) where needed. The latter test asks people to rate how tense they feel, for example, both in general (trait) and at that time (state). This information will be supplemented with that obtained from interviews and observations.

EVALUATION.

Personality inventories have the advantage of being quick to administer compared with other methods of assessment. They are also quick to score (most can be computer-scored nowadays), objective, and provide an easy way of comparing responses of the client with the average in the population. Well-designed personality tests should also have good reliability and validity. For example, the Beck Depression inventory has a reasonable reliability correlation of 0.73 (Beck et al. 1988) and accords with ratings of severity of depression given by psychiatrists. MMPI scales also relate well to clinical diagnoses.

The problem, as already indicated, is that their purpose is obvious to the client, who may then be able to fake responses. This type of problem, and the problem of response sets, can be solved to some extent by the use of specially designed test items to identify when this is happening. A more difficult problem is that in many cases clients may not have sufficient self-knowledge to give useful information about themselves. They may also respond in socially desirable ways – especially to items such as 'I go to a party every week'. Furthermore, not all characteristics are in fact stable over time (Mischel 1968); this makes it difficult to tell if the change observed is real or due to the test being unreliable. These tests may also not be culturally fair. In Puerto Rico it would not be considered abnormal to respond 'true' to the statement (included in the MMPI) 'evil spirits possess me at times' (Rogler et al. 1989).

Projective techniques provide a different approach to the assessment of personality. Rather than requiring the client to choose a response from a set of options, projective techniques present clients with unstruc-tured material to respond to as they see fit. Based on psychodynamic principles, it is assumed that they will 'project' aspects of their personality into the response. For example, the Rorschach test (1921) requires the client to look at a series of 'ink blots' such as that shown in Figure 2.2, and to describe what each depicts. The responses are then analysed with the aid of a test manual according to the nature of the

Figure 2.2 **Rorschach ink blots**

images described and the style of the responses (e.g. whether the client responds to the whole design or just part of it). Computer-generated interpretations are now available for certain Rorschach scores, making interpretation more objective. Another test is the Thematic Apperception Test or TAT (Murray 1971), which consists of a series of ambiguous pictures. In this case, the client is asked to make up a story about what is happening in each picture. Clients may also be asked to complete sentences, or to draw figures; this latter is particularly useful with children.

EVALUATION.

The Rorschach and the TAT are among the 10 most popular psychological tests. However, they present problems when it comes to interpretation. In reliability studies, different clinicians have been found to give different scores to the same responses, and although there are now standardised procedures for scoring the tests, they are not widely accepted (Kline 1993). Trained clinicians using modern standardised versions can achieve high interrater reliability. However, Smith and Dumont (1995) found that 14% of the clinicians they sampled, who had no training in the use of projective tests, nevertheless used them to make diagnostic and aetiological inferences. Eighty-seven per cent of those who did so produced inferences that had no scientific basis.

Some support is available for the validity of projective tests. Compared with questionnaires, projective tests allow the client freedom of expression. They also have the advantage that faking of responses is difficult. Erdberg and Exner (1984) found the predicted increase in inanimate movement responses (e.g. seeing flames flickering), which are indicators of anxiety, in those awaiting surgery. However, the tests may also lack validity, for two reasons. First, the results do not always agree with independent judgements about the client made in other ways; second, some may be biased against minority groups, because the materials used may not be appropriate (e.g. the TAT does not have any pictures of minority group members).

Conclusion

To conclude, there are clearly a variety of different ways in which the clinician can obtain the information needed in order to make informed decisions about the client. These methods differ in their utility according to the nature of the client, and also vary in terms of the key criteria of reliability and validity. The model of mental disorder adopted by the clinician will also affect the choice of method; a behavioural model would suggest an observational approach, for example, and a psychodynamic model an interview. Choice and utilisation of method, as well as putting information together and making a decision about the client, involve the clinician in an interpretative process that can easily lead to errors.

Progress exercise

(i) Which methods of assessment – interviews, observations or psychometric tests – would you use to assess the following areas of a client's functioning?:

Case history; cognitive functioning; neuropsychological functioning; personality/mood; behaviour; social functioning.

Give examples of assessment instruments where you can.

(ii) Draw up a chart to show the advantages and disadvantages of the different methods of assessment outlined above.

Evaluation of classification and diagnosis

In previous sections we have explained the potential value of classification and diagnosis. Here we will be considering the scientific status of the existing systems and procedures, and the difficulties that may arise whenever classification systems are used. The first section, then, is a specific critique, whereas the second makes more general points.

Criticisms of the existing systems of classification

Blashfield and Draguns (1976) suggest that four criteria can be used for evaluation: coverage; reliability; **descriptive validity**; predictive validity. To these, we can add **aetiological validity**. We will consider each of these in turn.

Coverage

This refers to the idea that the categories included in the system should cover all of those who are in need of help. Early versions of DSM had good coverage, because the categories were so vague. The later versions have stricter criteria for each category, but needed to have more categories overall. DSM IV defines disorders in terms of observable symptoms that are more precisely described than in previous systems. This makes the categories more homogeneous but reduces coverage. Perhaps because of this, it also has several residual categories (such as 'psychotic disorder not otherwise specified'), often referred to as 'wastebasket categories' for cases that do not fit the system. For some categories, such as dissociative disorders, most patients receive 'not otherwise specified' (NOS) diagnoses (Mezzich et al. 1989). This indicates that the fit between clients and system is not particularly good. There are also codes (rather than categories) available for disorders that do not fit into the system, such as problems related to an unwanted pregnancy. DSM has V codes and ICD has Z codes.

Problems are also caused by the fact that many of the symptoms of mental disorder are also evident in the normal population. Depression and obsessive behaviours are obvious examples. The issue of cut-off points, raised in Chapter 1, has not been resolved, nor does it seem likely that it ever will be.

Reliability

In order for the classification system to be seen as reliable, different clinicians should assign a given client to the same category. In general, agreement between clinicians about what a client's main difficulties are and how they are maintained has been found to be poor, even when they are given the same data about the client (Fewtrell 1981). Overlap between categories, and the fact that cases that fit the criteria exactly are rare, does not make the task any easier (Kendell 1975).

However, specific studies carried out on DSM have shown that it is increasing in reliability. For example, Beck et al., (1962) asked four clinicians to diagnose 153 patients independently, using DSM I, and found that only 54% of their diagnoses were the same. Kendell (1975) found that if very specific categories were used for classification, reliability was as low as 32% in some cases. Since then, successive versions of DSM have attempted to clarify the categories and provide more specific, objective criteria for inclusion. In 1985, Lipton and Simon were still able to show that 75% of 131 cases were given different diagnoses by clinicians in one American hospital (i.e. agreement was 25%). However, looking at a different behaviour, Di Nardo et al. (1993) reported around 70% agreement using DSM III and IIIR. The APA (1994) claim that version IV is more reliable than this, as a result of redrafting criteria for the categories that earlier research had shown to be particularly unreliable.

Other studies have explored the differences in reliability of different categories. Davison and Neale (1994) reported that the correlation between clinicians ranged from 0.92 for psychosexual disorders down to 0.54 for somatoform disorders, so there is clearly still a difference in reliability between categories. Nathan and Langenbucher (1999) reported that the reliability of a few categories (conduct disorder and substance abuse) had increased, but there had been no improvements in personality disorder (Axis II), and Axis I sleep, childhood and some schizophrenic disorders. Holmes (1994) found increased reliability using decision trees and computer programs to eliminate subjective bias on the part of clinicians.

Some researchers have argued that the lack of reliability just outlined may not be as bad as it seems. Falek and Moser (1975), for example, made the point that medical diagnoses may not be any more reliable than those for mental disorders, reporting only a 66% agreement for the cause of death on death certificates (signed by two different doctors). This, however, is hardly reassuring, and Klein et al. (1993) consider that further research is still required before DSM can be assumed to be acceptably reliable.

Another point to bear in mind here is cultural variation. For example, it has been shown (WHO 1973) that a diagnosis of schizophrenia was more likely to be given in Soviet Russia and in America than in the UK. Copeland et al. (1971) found that within the UK the age and location of clinicians affected the diagnosis, with older, Glasgow-trained clinicians giving higher ratings for abnormal behaviour than younger, London-trained ones. This highlights the need for continuing training. Training clinicians in the use of specific criteria and standardised interviews has been found to improve agreement (Okasha et al. 1993).

The system also seems to be applied in different ways to people from non-Western cultures. For example, schizophrenia seems to be overdiagnosed in West Indian and Asian immigrants to Britain. There are several reasons why this might be the case, as we shall see in Chapter 4, including the possibility that the difference accurately represents a different prevalence of schizophrenia in those ethnic groups. However, Garb (1997) found that when the amount and severity of symptoms were controlled, the difference was still observed, with African-American and Hispanic clients being more likely than whites to be diagnosed as schizophrenic. This indicates a diagnostic bias in this case.

It has also been found that females are more likely than males to be diagnosed with histrionic and dependent personality disorders and depression, and males are more likely to be diagnosed with antisocial personality disorder and obsessive-compulsive disorder (Becker & Lamb 1994). This is found with both male and female clinicians (Adler et al. 1990). It may occur because some behaviours that are part of the traditional gender role for males or females are mentioned in the diagnostic criteria – for example, submissiveness and dependency are traditionally female behaviours, but are mentioned as important features of dependent personality disorder. Thus sexism in the categories themselves may be responsible for the observed differences in prevalence.

Now we will move on to look at issues of validity; remember, however, that if the system is not reliable it cannot be valid.

Descriptive validity

This depends on the categories themselves being homogeneous, and the symptoms being different from those of other categories. DSM IV operates in terms of 'prototypes'; it acknowledges that some features of disorders will be the same in different cases, but that others will vary. Hence it has a list of criteria for each disorder, of which a certain number must be evident, while others may or may not be present. Given this, it is not surprising that the categories are not homogeneous. Schizophrenics, for example, differ so widely that it is difficult to see what they have in common, and DSM has several subgroups for the category.

Individuals with different diagnoses may also show similar symptoms – depression may be seen in some anxiety disorders and in manic depression, for example. In fact, most patients do show **comorbidity** (Kessler et al. 1994), meaning that they have several disorders at once. If disorders are prone to occur together, it raises questions about whether they are in fact separate disorders. Disorders most likely to be associated with comorbidity include depression, substance abuse, anxiety and personality disorders.

One way of trying to assess this type of validity is by comparing DSM categories against clinical judgement in field trials, and many of these were carried out prior to the publication of DSM IV. Spitzer et al. (1989) asked large numbers of clinicians to rate clients on various criteria to see if they could agree on what was important. As a result, a proposed new category of self-defeating personality disorder was rejected, as it could not be clearly distinguished from the existing categories. However, Pope et al. (1999) sampled 367 American psychiatrists, asking if they thought that Dissociative Identity Disorder should be included as a category in DSM IV. Only about a quarter felt that there was scientific evidence for its validity. However, this reference to clinical judgement as a criterion is a very limited form of validity – how do we know that clinical judgement is valid in the first place? We will return to this in the next chapter; for the time being, it is sufficient to note that for descriptive validity to be established it is more important to show that the category is distinct from others in terms of symptoms, causes and treatments.

Predictive validity

This depends on the categories having predictive value in terms of the future course of the disorder, and has yet to be investigated fully. Heather (1976) pointed out that there is only a 50% chance of predicting which treatment will be given from the diagnosis. In some cases, there is evidence of predictive validity. For example, many schizophrenics improve when given neuroleptic drugs, whereas other types of client do not. Depressive clients respond well to electroconvulsive shock therapy; schizophrenics do not.

Aetiological validity

This requires that all patients who have the same diagnosis should have developed the disorder for the same reason(s). This is clearly not the case. For example, schizophrenia would appear to have a genetic basis in some cases; in others, however, there is no evidence of a family history of the problem. Such differences may be the result of inadequacies in the diagnostic system. It is also possible that this type of validity is unattainable, simply because there are generally multiple causes for disorders.

DSM may also fail to be valid cross-culturally; Littlewood (1992) argues that Axis V of DSM IV makes ethnocentric (i.e. white Western) assumptions about the nature of family life, work and education. Lewis-Fernandez (1997) has criticised the fourth revision of DSM for ignoring the recommendations of the National Institute of Mental Health Committeee on Culture and Diagnosis as regards dissociative disorders, for example. Of the 36 recommendations aimed at taking cultural diversity into account, only 42% were included in the final version, and 'critique of the universality of DSM IV diagnoses was not tolerated' (Lewis-Fernandez 1997, p. 385). The implication of this is that they are considered to be applicable world-wide. This will be discussed further in Chapter 4.

Rosenhan's study

Finally, in a very well-known study called 'On being sane in insane places', Rosenhan (1973) presented evidence that relates to the issue of validity (see Chapter 6 for more details of this study and a critique).

The study was asking whether clinicians could reliably distinguish the sane from the insane. Remember that if they cannot do this, the system cannot be valid either, since reliability is a prerequisite for validity.

Briefly, Rosenhan's researchers presented themselves to admissions officers at psychiatric hospitals, claiming to hear voices but otherwise behaving as they normally would. They were admitted (mostly with a diagnosis of schizophrenia) and behaved normally once inside the hospital. Staff, however, interpreted their normal behaviours in ways consistent with the diagnosis. Writing notes, for example, was seen as pathological behaviour, and pacing the corridors as nervousness rather than boredom. It took the hospitals concerned 7–52 days to discharge the pseudopatients.

In a parallel study, staff were warned that 'fake' patients might try to gain admission to the hospital, and were asked to assess whether or not new patients were likely to be fakes (in fact there were no fake patients). Around 20% of new patients were assessed as fakes by at least one member of staff. This study shows that, in 1973 at any rate, staff could be deceived, and did find it difficult to discriminate between normal and mentally disordered individuals in a psychiatric hospital. However, as Kety (1974) has pointed out, using a fake blood capsule to simulate vomiting blood would hardly be a fair test of medical ability to diagnose the source of the blood. Similarly, faking the symptoms of mental disorder is not a fair test of clinicians' ability to diagnose that condition. However, the study does still demonstrate the clinicians' inability to assess the accurate information that was presented subsequently.

Compared with the data available on DSM IV, there are very few for ICD 10. However, it is thought that ICD 10 is an improvement on its predecessors and probably quite similar to DSM IV, although DSM is more specific in categories and symptomatology, and therefore probably more reliable (Costello et al. 1995). Sartorius et al. (1995) reported from field trials that interrater reliability was particularly high for schizophrenia and substance abuse, but less good for personality disorders.

Practical issues regarding classification

Clinical bias

As implied in the definition of reliability, whatever the system in use for classification, it has to contend with the biases and limitations of the clinicians using it. At the outset, they may have different styles of interviewing and information-gathering, as noted earlier. Clinicians have been shown to pay more attention to data gathered earlier in the process than to later data (Meehl 1960), and McCoy (1976) found that they put more weight on information from some sources (such as parents, rather than children, for example). Clinicians may expect people that they see to be abnormal, and overemphasise information that supports this idea (called the 'reading-in syndrome' by Phares 1979). They also have personal biases relating to age, race, socio-economic status and gender (Strakowski et al. 1995). Political use of diagnosis as a form of social control may also influence decision-making processes (Littlewood & Lipsedge 1989). These aspects will be explored more fully in Chapter 4.

Medical basis

Many psychologists are also unhappy about the assumption inherent in the classification systems that mental disorders may prove to be biologically based and are therefore to be treated medically. This includes those who subscribe to the humanistic, psychodynamic, cognitive-behavioural, systemic and constructionist models mentioned in Chapter 1. Szasz (1962) took this point further in his argument that there is no such thing as mental illness, because illness can only affect the body, not the mind. In practice, many clinicians have objected that DSM does not provide practical guidance about treatment (Jampala et al. 1986). Lindsay and Powell (1994) further point out that DSM ignores functional analysis, which is an important part of many behavioural interventions used by psychologists.

Categories or dimensions?

The use of categories, rather than dimensions, has also been criticised (Lindsay & Powell 1994) on the basis that attempting to create clear-cut categories may be attempting to tidy up human behaviour too much. In practice, people are much too complex for this to be feasible. Most behaviours are in fact normally distributed in the population (i.e. are dimensional) rather than being **bimodal** (i.e. in categories such as normal/abnormal). The argument for dimensions is still ongoing, but of course it has to face the problem of deciding on the appropriate dimensions to use. It may not prove to be appropriate for all disorders either (Carr 1999), since some may be dimensional (e.g. mental retardation) while others appear to be categorical (e.g. dyslexia).

Individuals or systems?

A final point is that the current classification systems rely on the individual as the unit of analysis. The client is often seen and assessed in isolation from social influences. Some clinicians, especially those who adopt a family systems approach, regard this as inappropriate because the behaviour forms part of a complex pattern of interaction between individuals, and cannot be understood in isolation.

Ethical issues regarding classification

In some instances, the use of classification and diagnosis can be seen to be harmful; this may be the case whether it is used correctly or incorrectly.

Legal aspects

The first issue to consider is the legal consequences of the procedure. Although it is less common than it used to be now that care in the community is the norm, it is still possible under the Mental Health Act (1983) for individuals to be compulsorily detained in a psychiatric hospital. Commitment orders can be from 3 days to 6 months, and can include a provision for treatment (although only emergency treatment can be given without the patient's consent). Sectioned individuals also lose some rights (such as voting rights), and they are excluded from jury service and from holding gun licences.

As regards criminal law, in Britain individuals classified as suffering from a mental disorder can be judged incompetent to stand trial for criminal offences under the Criminal procedure (insanity and unfitness to plead) Act (1991). This is an uncommon plea, and does not relate to ability to give evidence in court. They have to prove that they are incapable of doing at least one of the following:

- instructing counsel;
- appreciating the significance of their plea;
- challenging a juror;
- examining a witness;
- understanding and following evidence.

Even if sane at the time of the trial, they can put forward an insanity defence if they can convince the court that they were insane at the time of the crime. This goes back to the McNaughten (or M'Naghten) rules of 1843, which excuse the individual from responsibility if he can show that he did not know the act was wrong or was unaware of its nature. Again, this is rarely applied, as few people are disordered enough to qualify. A plea of diminished responsibility can also be presented in murder cases, under the Homicide Act (1957). It allows the sentence to be reduced or a hospital order made.

Clearly, there can be a great deal to gain by doing this, although Szasz has noted the case of Joe Skulski, who was judged unfit to plead but ended up spending more time in a psychiatric hospital than he would have spent in prison had he been found guilty of the offence. On the other hand, Peter Sutcliffe (the 'Yorkshire Ripper') had such pleas rejected and was sent to prison for his crimes, where he has been brutalised by the other inmates. In Britain most mentally disordered offenders do stand trial. If found guilty, psychiatric evidence is offered in mitigation pleas to alter the sentencing given; they may be sent to a secure psychiatric hospital rather than a prison.

Labelling aspects

Another ethical issue relates to the use of psychiatric diagnoses to persecute minority groups, as suggested by Szasz (1962). Soviet Russia, as mentioned earlier, used psychiatric labelling in order to marginalise those who objected to the political regime. Cochrane and Sashidharan (1995) argue that the systems in use at present assume that the white, Western norms of behaviour should be followed by all, and that those who depart from these norms require treatment. As Scheff (1966) states: 'Far from being culture-free . . . symptoms are themselves offenses against implicit understandings of particular cultures' (p. 65). On the other hand, Lopez and Hernandez (1986) have suggested that clinicians may overreact and take too much account of subcultural norms, thereby minimising the potential seriousness of the client's disorder. This will be discussed further in Chapter 4.

Laypersons and professionals alike may favour diagnoses on the grounds that they provide an explanation for behaviour that is otherwise difficult to understand (e.g. referring to a murderer as a 'psychopath'), but this is clearly not the case; they are only shorthand descriptions. Similarly, it has been argued that the diagnosis can be unhelpful for the client, in that the responsibility for behaviour is then taken away – it is the disorder that makes them behave in that way, and the doctors or psychiatrists have responsibility for treatment. There may even be a tendency to adopt the role suggested by the diagnosis, which could prevent recovery (Parsons 1951) as it would then become a self-fulfilling prophecy.

Finally, such diagnostic labels may themselves have negative effects on the way that mentally disordered persons are viewed and treated by others. This was demonstrated in the study by Rosenhan discussed earlier. The labelling theory of deviance (Becker 1963) has been applied to mental disorder by Scheff (1966), who considers that once labelled, people are then rewarded when they behave in ways that fit in with stereotypes associated with the label, and punished when they do not. Thus only disordered behaviour is reinforced. Langer and Abelson (1974) found that clinicians watching a video of a person labelled as a job applicant rated him as better adjusted than did those who saw the same video with the person labelled as a patient. The stigma associated with such labels (Goffman 1968) may also lead to the individual losing employment, home and social support (Bean & Mounser 1993). With potential consequences such as these, it is doubly important that the system in use is thoroughly researched and appropriately used, and that the benefits outweigh the costs to the individual.

Chapter summary

In this chapter we have looked at the background to the two modern classification systems for mental disorder, DSM and ICD. The five axes specified in DSM (clinical syndromes, personality disorders and mental retardation, general medical conditions, psychosocial and environmental problems, and a global assessment of functioning) have been described. A more detailed description has been given of the presenting symptoms and diagnostic criteria for five major conditions – schizophrenia, major depression, obsessive-compulsive disorder, bulimia nervosa, and antisocial personality disorder – together with a case study for each. The ICD system has also been presented and the main similarities and differences between it and DSM have been described.

In the second part of the chapter we have outlined the important principles of scientific assessment, with particular emphasis on reliability and validity. Methods used as part of the diagnostic process were then explored, including clinical interviews, observations and psychometric tests. All of these were described and linked to the different areas of functioning that the clinician might explore, including case history, cognitive and neuropsychological functioning, personality, behaviour and social functioning. The reliability and validity of the different methods has been discussed. Finally, the classification systems in current use have themselves been evaluated in terms of their reliability and validity, and the practical and ethical implications of correct and incorrect diagnoses. Overall, it has been concluded that classification is an inexact process, but it may nevertheless have considerable benefits for people who do have recognisable syndromes of disturbed behaviour.

Consider each of the five case studies presented in the first part of the chapter in the light of the five DSM axes, and present as full a diagnosis as you can. If possible, ask a friend to do the same task, and compare the reliability of your diagnosis.

Review exercise

73

Further reading

Clipson, C. & Steer, J. (1998) *Case studies in Abnormal Psychology*. Boston: Houghton Mifflin. (Sixteen case studies with a detailed account of presenting symptoms, background, criteria for diagnosis, treatment and outlook, all written in a very accessible style.)

Comer, R.J. (1998) *Abnormal Psychology*. New York: Freeman. (Gives detailed evaluation of different methods of assessment.)

Frude, N. (1998). *Understanding Abnormal Psychology*. Oxford: Blackwell. (Detailed, readable account of almost all of the categories of mental disorder.)

3

Multiple personality disorder (MPD)

What is MPD?
Case studies
Origins of MPD
Evaluation: spontaneous or iatrogenic?

What is MPD?

Diagnosis

The classification system ICD 10 has a group of disorders entitled 'Neurotic, stress-related and somatoform disorders'. DSM IV has a group called 'Dissociative disorders', in which there is a disruption in 'consciousness, memory, identity or perception of the environment' (APA 1994, p. 477). Both groups include multiple personality disorder (MPD, also known as dissociative identity disorder) as well as various amnesic states.

MPD is characterised by a lack of integration of different aspects of consciousness, which means that the individual demonstrates several different sub-personalities or identities (known as '**alters**') at different times. Cases have been reported with as few as 2 identities and as many as 4500, the average number being 15 for women and 8 for men (APA 1994). These identities will vary in terms of their names, personality characteristics, age and even gender from the primary personality (that by which the individual is most commonly known). They may switch gradually, but the changeover is often abrupt, and the personalities may interrupt one another. Stress may prompt a change from one identity to another. Some identities will be aware of the others, but they do not all have this awareness. The primary identity is often guilt-ridden, passive, depressed and dependent, while the others may be aggressive and outgoing.

Amnesia for personal activities, both long and short term, is common. Thus one identity may not remember something that happened when another identity was in control. In some cases, amnesia may cover an extended period of childhood, and may be linked with physical and/or sexual abuse. Flashbacks and self-mutilation may occur, and present relationships may be abusive ones. The diagnostic criteria from DSM IV are given in Box 3.1.

BOX 3.1 Diagnostic criteria for multiple personality disorder (APA 1994)

1. Presence of two or more personalities, each with a different way of perceiving, relating to and thinking about the self and the environment.
2. Behaviour is controlled on different occasions by at least two of these personalities.
3. Extensive forgetting of important personal information.
4. Cannot be explained by effects of substance abuse, medical conditions or (in the case of children) fantasy play.

Measurement

In 1986 Bernstein and Putnam produced the first test to measure MPD, called the Dissociative Experiences Scale; this was revised in 1993. More recent scales include the questionnaire of Experiences of Dissociation (Riley 1988) and the Dissociative Questionnaire (Vanderlinden et al. 1991). These are all based on the client's response to a set of questions (the DES contains 28, for example) and can be used for routine screening or initial tentative diagnoses. The client is asked to decide what percentage of the time they have certain experiences, when not under the influence of drugs or alcohol. Experiences include finding unfamiliar things among their belongings, suddenly realising that they cannot remember part of a journey they have just made, failing to recognise people they know, and being shown that they have done something that they have no memory of at all. Other questions involve feelings of depersonalisation – feeling that their bodies are not their own, or that they are standing outside and observing themselves. Out of a possible final score of 100, Carlson and Putnam (1993) found that normal adults score about 4, schizophrenics 20, post-traumatic stress patients 31 and MPD patients 57. College students, incidentally, score about 14 – often attributed to regular daydreaming! Carlson and Putnam (1993) suggested that the cut-off point should be a score of 30, on the grounds that 80% of diagnosed multiples score over 30, and 80% of non-multiples score under 30.

The existence of measurement instruments is an important require-ment for further research into this area, but two problems should be noted with these scales. First, results are easy to fake. Gilbertson et al. (1992) found that after instructing groups of student nurses to answer in different ways (normally, faking problems, faking good or faking MPD), they were easily able to produce the required results. Second, questionnaire scores have been subjected to **factor analysis**. This is a statistical technique that aims to show how many different factors (or clusters of behaviours) underlie responses to questions. In this case, factor analysis of scores from the various different questionnaires available has been shown to yield anything from 3 to 7 factors. Since those found in different studies are not always the same, it has been concluded that there may be as many as 11 factors being measured on the scales (Hacking 1995). To quote Hacking (1995, p. 112): 'a problem arises when it seems to many observers that "dissociative experiences" is used to refer to a great many experiences that have singularly little in common with one another'.

History

Bearing in mind the problems of assessment, we can turn next to look at historical changes in the frequency of multiple personality disorder. The prevalence of the disorder has been assessed at different times and in different parts of the world. Perhaps the earliest case was described by Ellenberger, a German physician, in 1791. In 1816, Mary Reynolds was described as a case of 'double consciousness' (Mitchill 1817), but it was not until 1876 that the first systematic study was undertaken. This was of Felida X, whose case was identified by the researcher, Azam, as a case of 'dedoublement de la personnalité' (double or split personality). Felida was reported to have two personalities, as the term implies; in 1885, the case of Louis Vivet, who had eight distinct personalities, was reported in France. When this was published in England (Myers 1896), he was described as being a 'multiple personality'.

In general, little evidence of MPD was found in the early 20th century. There was also a loss of interest in hysteria, with which it had been associated. Early multiples tended to show hysterical symptoms such as paralysis, and somatic symptoms, and MPD was viewed as a subtype of hysteria. Freud contributed significantly to this lack of interest when he abandoned his **seduction theory** – the idea that hysteria was caused by childhood sexual abuse – on the basis that the reports he obtained from patients were fantasies rather than reality.

In the literature up to 1944, just 76 cases were reported in the medical literature (Taylor & Martin 1944). Between 1944 and 1969, 14 cases were reported (Greaves 1980). By 1970 only 100 cases had been reported in professional journals. However, by 1986 around 6000 patients had been diagnosed (Coons 1986) and it was being described as an epidemic of multiple personality. By 1990 there were thousands in America and Canada (Mersky 1995). Acocella (1999) reports that there were almost 40,000 new cases between 1985 and 1995. Ross et al. (1991) estimated that 2% of the North American population may be affected (cited in Hacking 1995, p. 108), and the prevalence certainly appears to be on the increase. There is now an International Society for the Study of Multiple Personality and Dissociation (ISSMP & D).

There is also considerable cultural variation in prevalence of MPD. The rate of occurrence of MPD is very much higher in North America than in Britain. Ross et al. (1991) screened 299 psychiatric patients in Canada and found a 3.3% prevalence in that group. Modestin (1992) in Switzerland calculated from a survey of psychiatrists that 0.05–0.1% of patients were affected. MPD has been reported as virtually unknown in Czechoslovakia, New Zealand, Australia and India. In India, however, 'possession syndrome' (being taken over by the spirit of a dead relative) is quite common, and could be seen as a cultural variation of MPD (Adityanjee & Khandelwal 1989), as could 'Zar', a similar syndrome found in the Sudan (Boddy 1989).

Evaluation: reasons for variations in prevalence

How can these historical and cultural variations be explained? There are four possibilities that we will consider here:

- changes and biases in the diagnostic system;
- changes and biases in clinicians;
- cultural causation;
- social constructionism.

The first two explanations relate to the concept of MPD as an **iatrogenic** disorder, meaning that it is induced in the patient by the psychiatric system itself. The third suggests that it is spontaneous or genuine. The fourth argues that it may well be a combination of these, a collusion between the system and the person in difficulties.

Changes and biases in the diagnostic system

It is clear that MPD has not always been recognised as a disorder in the past, not even in previous versions of DSM. It was not until 1980 that it was officially recognised in DSM IV. As DSM has become more specific in its description of MPD, it might be expected that clinicians might become more confident in diagnosing it, leading to an apparent increase in general prevalence compared with that observed in the past. There may also be variability between cultures according to the training given to clinicians. However, it may also be the case that cultural variation is the result of behaviours shown by MPD patients being an accepted part of everyday life in some cultures (Lewis-Fernandez 1997) and hence not being regarded as requiring psychiatric help, or not being given the same label – 'possession syndrome' being a good example of this. Many culturally accepted healing rituals and religious practices in other cultures involve trance states. Lewis-Fernandez (1997) argues that these have not been differentiated in the present version of DSM from pathological states. MPD may be a genuine 'culture-bound syndrome' (see Chapter 4) or it may simply be that it is only viewed as a problem in some Western countries.

It may also be possible to query the validity of MPD as a diagnostic category (North et al. 1993). Most MPD patients also meet the criteria for other disorders – at least 3–4 according to North et al. (1993) and

11 according to Ross (1995). These include depression (90%), substance abuse (57%), antisocial personality and borderline personality disorder (64%) (Acocella 1999). Boon and Draijer (1993), in Holland, found that many of their sample of 71 had had other diagnoses before; for example, they may have been diagnosed as schizophrenic because they reported hearing voices. In a survey of psychiatrists, Pope et al. (1999) found that only 20% felt that there was good evidence for MPD's validity as a category. Most felt that it rarely occurs spontaneously without prompting.

Changes and biases in clinicians

The second proposal is that MPD may be the result of clinical bias. Increasing awareness of the syndrome through the development of clear clinical criteria may have had the effect of oversensitising clinicians, in this view. A change of mood, clothing or hairstyle could then be misinterpreted by the clinician as the emergence of an alter. When provided with suggestible patients, it may be possible for clinicians to encourage patients to show behaviours appropriate to MPD. In fact such patients have been found to be more hypnotisable than most, and may be able to go into trances spontaneously without the use of hypnosis (e.g. through the use of guided imagery, a technique in which patients are guided through a fantasy by the clinician). In such states they may be more open to leading questions and suggestions from the clinician. Spanos (1994) has pointed out that the diagnostic interviews (described in a later section of the chapter) carried out for MPD contain all the information needed by the patient in order to produce the basic signs of the disorder. Interestingly, Ross et al. (1989) found that of 236 cases they surveyed, the mean number of alters was 16 – exactly the number shown by the most famous case, Sybil. Patients may also be generally vulnerable people, as shown by the fact that many have other disorders as well (comorbidity). For example, Acocella (1999) found that 61% have attempted suicide, 20% have worked as prostitutes and 12% have criminal records.

The high prevalence of the disorder in some countries, such as Holland for example, has been attributed to the frequent visits of North American experts to that country in the past (Aldridge-Morris 1989). It is argued that within a culture, a relatively small number of clinicians may be responsible for a large number of diagnoses. Thigpen and

Cleckley (1984), who originally reported the well-known case of Eve (see later) have stated that they very rarely see such cases. In Modestin's (1992) study of Swiss psychiatrists, it was noted that the patients were not evenly distributed: 3 of the 770 psychiatrists surveyed saw a lot more MPD patients than the others. In Baltimore, America, Ross (1992) found that the numbers of MPD patients at one centre rose by 900% after an MPD expert joined the staff. Thus Acocella (1999, p. 54) concludes, 'Just as some exotic syndromes are confined to Japan, or certain South Sea Islands, [MPD] is a syndrome geographically related to high concentration zones of therapists who identify with the beliefs of a particular psychological sub-culture.' In other words, clinical bias may be responsible for the observed variations in prevalence.

Further evidence pertaining to this view can be derived from an examination of what happens when patients refuse to accept that they have MPD. That some therapists are reluctant to accept that the patient does *not* have MPD is evident in some of the terms they use. 'Stonewalling', for example, is the term for a patient's refusal to accept the diagnosis, and it is generally regarded as a poor prognostic sign (i.e. an indication that they will not make good progress in treatment). Claims by patients that they made up all the information given are viewed as 'resistance' to treatment (Putnam et al. 1986). Acocella (1999, p. 99) provides the following example: 'One patient reports that when she finally told Ault [the therapist] that she had never been abused, that the memories were false, he replied "Which personality am I talking to now?".'

Cultural causation

This explanation for cultural differences in prevalence argues that the observed cases of MPD are genuine (or 'spontaneous'), and that the characteristics of certain cultures are such that they bring about the disorder. It has been suggested for example (Erikson 1976) that there are four aspects of modern living that make traumatic neuroses of all kinds more likely, because they induce a state of chronic trauma and uncertainty. These are:

- lack of clear moral guidelines;
- lack of control over life;
- sensory overload;
- being disconnected from other people.

Similarly, Martinez-Taboas (1991) argues that MPD is more likely in societies in which the individual is viewed as a separate self (individualistic societies), rather than community-based or collectivist societies. Kluft (1998) describes MPD as perhaps more properly termed 'multiple *reality* disorder', to emphasise that it may be the result of such confusions. Such theories, however, are difficult to test empirically.

Social constructionism

The final explanation is that proposed by the social constructionists. In this view, the problem is neither spontaneous nor iatrogenic. Hartocollis (1998) argues that it is not iatrogenic in the sense of being artificially manufactured by the suggestions of the therapist, or the result of a false diagnosis, nor is the suffering of the patient in doubt. What is 'manufactured' is the way that experience is dissected by Western culture, and in particular psychiatrists. This could account for historical changes in the way the disorder is expressed. For example, Kenny (1986) has pointed out that the early cases had just two personalities, corresponding to the Christian dualism of good and evil. Modern cases have many confused selves, corresponding to the variety of possibilities offered by modern life.

In this view, developments in psychology, as well as developments in society, have gone hand-in-hand to create the epidemic. Among other things, the development of the media in Western society has led to an interest in role-playing(Varma et al. 1981), as well as an awareness of different possible identities. According to Acocella (1999) 'we are exposed to illusory representations far more vivid than our own lives' (p. 50). Acocella notes that the increase in MPD parallels the increase in availability of TV remote controls, and suggests that the multiples are 'channel-surfing' (p. 48). The internet allows people to adopt an on-line persona, and there are web sites for multiples that provide plenty of information about the problem. Television, too, provides models, and following revelations in the Oprah Winfrey show (a well-known American chat show), Kluft (1998) has suggested that MPD could also be regarded as 'Oprahgenic' in its origins.

In psychology, there has been a revival of interest in hypnosis in recent years, and in some parts of the world increasing disposable income has facilitated the development of the private psychotherapy business. As cognitive-behavioural therapies have grown in popularity, so the lengthier, psychodynamically oriented therapies have suffered (especially in state hospitals, where they would not be regarded as cost-effective). MPD could be seen as offering them some scope for development, because psychodynamic explanations and treatments, as we shall see later, have proved to be the most popular way of dealing with MPD. The standard treatment, according to Acocella (1999), would cost around 17,000 dollars a year, even after the contribution from insurance companies. This would make such therapists into good money-spinners. The group that mostly patronises such therapists, in fact, consists of white North American females – precisely those who are most likely to be diagnosed with MPD.

Other developments in society in recent times that are relevant here are the rise of feminism and the increasing awareness of child abuse that accompanied it. These will be discussed in later sections when we look at explanations and treatments for the disorder. To conclude, a quote from Hacking (1995, p. 12): 'The fact that a certain type of mental illness appears only in specific historical or geographical contexts does not imply that it is manufactured, artificial, or in any other way not real.' Even if the disorder turns out to be an accepted, even fashionable, way of expressing distress, it is still important to deal with it in an appropriate manner. In the following sections we will look at how it has been dealt with to date. This will give us further clues as to its nature.

Case studies

Three cases will be discussed in this section: the case of Eve; the case of Sybil; and that of Billy Milligan. They have been selected because they all raise different, important issues about the nature of MPD.

Eve (Thigpen & Cleckley 1954)

Eve White was a 25-year-old married woman referred to a psychiatrist for treatment because she suffered from blinding headaches for which no physical cause could be found. On interview, marital conflicts, personal frustrations, blackouts and loss of memory were all revealed as well. Following a hypnosis session, her psychiatrist received a letter from her, with a note added that appeared to be from someone else – the handwriting was completely different. She subsequently denied sending the letter at all, but admitted to having heard voices. Her personality seemed to change at this point in the interview, and she announced herself as Eve Black ('Black' was Eve White's maiden name). This personality, in contrast to the serious, conventional, considerate and retiring Eve White, was carefree, mischievous, irresponsible, pleasure-seeking and lacking in depth of feeling. As Acocella (1999) puts it she was a 'vivacious party girl – leaving her host personality with unexplanied hangovers and a reputation in local bars' (p. 2). This good–bad split is a common feature of MPD cases.

Following the first spontaneous change, hypnosis had to be used to elicit Eve Black, but it became easier and easier for Eve Black to take over. While Eve Black was fully aware of, and rather despised, Eve White, Eve White had no knowledge of Eve Black (except for that gained during therapy) and no access to her consciousness. This is known as **asymmetrical amnesia**. Thus during childhood Eve Black would be disobedient, leaving Eve White to get the blame for something that she could not remember doing. Although her parents and husband had observed these changes, they did not interpret them as anything other than inconsistent behaviour. The skills shown by one (such as driving or sewing) could not be carried out by the other. One relative reported that Eve had been married prior to her present marriage. Eve White was unaware of this, but Eve Black eventually admitted it was true, and that her 'husband' had physically abused her. At such times she would allow Eve White to take over so that she would not suffer any pain, and then erase Eve White's memory for the beatings.

After 8 months of treatment, Eve White seemed to be gaining more control, at least in the work environment, but this began to change and blackouts became common again. Eve Black denied responsibility for these, and finally a third personality, known as Jane, emerged. Jane spoke with a different voice, and was considered to be more mature and capable than the other two. She was aware of both Eves, but could not displace Eve Black.

Psychometric and physiological tests were also given to the different personalities. Eve White obtained a higher score on the WAIS than Eve Black, but Eve Black's Rorschach results were considered to be psychologically healthier, indicating regression rather than repression. On the Semantic Differential (Osgood et al. 1957), which is a test of attitudes, there were clear differences between the three personalities. Eve White came out as socialised, with a normal view of the world but a negative view of self. Eve Black showed less stability over time, saw herself as perfect and the world as abnormal. Jane had the most healthy perception of both the world and herself. On the EEG, Eve White and Jane showed normal records, indistinguishable from one another; Eve Black, however, showed more signs of tension, with a slightly fast trace of a type sometimes associated with psychopathic personality. A later analysis of film footage (London et al. 1969) found that each personality showed a different pattern of eye movements. These pieces of evidence from objective tests indicate that there was a genuine difference in Eve's behaviour when different alters were in control. Such behavioural differences would be difficult to simulate.

Thigpen and Cleckley interpreted Eve's problems as being due to her feelings of rejection as a child, and anxiety about her role as a wife and mother. To escape from these problems, she took on the role of Eve Black to take her back to the period before she was married and allow her an opportunity to be free of responsibilities. Their aim in therapy was to develop Jane's personality so that she would be dominant, as her personality was felt to be better adjusted. However, a fourth personality, Evelyn, appeared some months later. She knew all about the other three, and was felt to be a more complete personality.

This is where the book and the film (*The Three Faces of Eve*) left the story. In 1975, a woman called Chris Sizemore revealed that she was the real 'Eve' and that she had in fact had 22 personalities over the years, the first occurring when she was just 2 years old. In 1989 in her book *A Mind of My Own*, she claimed that some of her alters had been present from birth because they were alters from a past life. When she was 46 years old, they spontaneously integrated into one personality.

Evaluation

Thigpen and Cleckley (1984) were not entirely convinced themselves that Eve was a geniune MPD case rather than a skilled actress, and they reported that in the 30 years that had elapsed since their study they had only come across one other case. Although the objective tests would seem to provide convincing evidence of her genuineness, they have been criticised by Orne et al. (1984). In many cases, for example, there were no control conditions employing people who had been asked to fake MPD. The extent to which the people assessing test results may have been biased by being told that they were from different people is also unclear.

According to Arrigo and Pezdek (1998), textbook versions have misrepresented the case by ignoring what they describe as 'the wretchedness of her condition' as regards her early experiences. At the age of 15, Eve eloped with a sexual sadist, and consequently suffered from frigidity and an eating disorder. She had attempted to strangle her own daughter, and subsequently faked integration of her personalities. Her later career as a lecturer, which earned her an award for public service in 1982, has also been ignored.

Sybil (Schreiber 1973)

Probably the best-known case of MPD, as a result of the Hollywood film of the same name, Sybil was actually studied by Cornelia Wilbur, an orthodox Freudian, but the case was rejected by scientific journals of the time and eventually written up as book by Schreiber, a journalist. Wilbur, a psychoanalyst, was interested in childhood trauma as the basis of MPD. Sybil Dorsett was referred for treatment in 1954 at the age of 31, because she was unable to account for substantial periods of time. Her problems began at the age of 22, with memory lapses and severe headaches. She also suffered from fugues, a condition in which the sufferer finds themselves in a strange place with no idea how they got there. Wilbur's treatment of Sybil took 2534 sessions over a period of 11 years, and involved sharing a house with her client at one stage. She claimed that Sybil had an IQ of 170. Wilbur used hypnosis and the drug sodium amytal (which increases hypnotic suggestibility) to access her client's early memories.

This eventually revealed no fewer than 16 alters, some of whom were children (including a baby called Ruthie – who split off after watching her parents have sex) and two who were the opposite sex (called Mike and Sid). They all had different images of how they looked, as well as different tastes in friends, food and music, and different skills (e.g. one could play the piano). It also revealed that Sybil had been sexually abused by her mother, who had administered cold water enemas which Sybil was prevented from expelling by being bound and hung upside down, She had also had various sharp objects stuck into her anus and vagina. The alters had been created, it was said, in order to cope with the abuse. They would take over, and Sybil would not remember what had happened. What was unusual about Sybil was not only the number of alters, but the fact that some were transsexual, i.e. alters of the opposite sex. The history of abuse also differentiated her from Eve who, although she had had childhood traumas, was never sexually assaulted. Because the case appeared at a time when child abuse was in the public consciousness, it found what Hartocollis (1998) describes as a 'cultural fit' in a way that Eve did not, and became the best-known case of MPD. Recently, Sybil was identified as Shirley Mason, from Minnesota, who died in 1998 aged 75.

Evaluation

This case, unlike that of Eve, was never written up in the professional journals where it could be subjected to peer review from other therapists. Wilbur, Schreiber and Sybil are all now dead, and cannot be questioned, but there are some criticisms available from those who worked with them. For example, Spiegel (interviewed by Acocella 1999) took over from Wilbur during a period of absence. He found that she had originally diagnosed Sybil as schizophrenic, but Schreiber wanted to write about a case of MPD. In fact Spiegel felt that Sybil was a case of hysteria. He also noticed that she was unusually hypnotisable, to the extent that she entered trances spontaneously. When she was in trances, Wilbur gave her different names, and the multiples developed from there. Spiegel narrates an interview with Sybil in which she asks if he wants her to be Helen, adding that Wilbur would have wanted that when talking about the issue under consideration. When Spiegel says that she can be Sybil if she would prefer, she agrees; 'Fine, I'd prefer it that way' (Acocella p. 56).

Another critic is Rieber (1999) who obtained 2 hours of taped conversations between Schreiber and Wilbur about Sybil. In the course of the conversations, Wilbur mentioned that she had to list the names of alters for Sybil to get her to respond appropriately. She also used hypnotic suggestions and powerful drugs such as sodium pentothal. Schreiber mentions at one point a letter from Sybil in which she denies everything that she claimed had happened to her. Even before this, in 1987, Miller commented (p. 348) that 'Sybil's life was made up by Sybil, her doctor, when she became a case, and again, when she became a book, by her author. Sixteen selves were imagined, but it is not even entirely certain that there were as many as two.'

Billy Milligan (Keyes 1981)

This is another case that has been written up by a non-academic; Keyes was a novelist and teacher of English. Known as 'the Campus Rapist', Milligan came to the public attention because he was arrested after a series of three rapes carried out in 1977 in Ohio State University. The evidence against him was overwhelming – handcuffs and weapons were found at his flat, as well as the credit cards of victims, and he was identified from fingerprints and mugshots. Initially, he was diagnosed as a schizophrenic with an IQ of 68 and considered unfit to stand trial. Cornelia Wilbur was called in, however, and diagnosed him as a case of MPD. Milligan entered a plea of not guilty on the grounds that one of his alters (Adalana, the lesbian) had committed the crimes. He reported 24 personalities, three of whom were female, with nationalities that included British, Australian and Yugoslavian, and backgrounds ranging from criminal to weapons experts and lesbian poets. More details are given in Box 3.2 of some of the alters. Others were felt to be undesirable and were suppressed by Arthur, the dominant alter who decided who should be allowed to 'hold the spot'.

BOX 3.2 Some of Billy Milligan's alters

BILLY (26): the core personality, a high school dropout.

ARTHUR (22): English, rational, emotionless, wore glasses and read Arabic. A capitalist and an atheist. He dominated the others (except when the situation was dangerous) and decided who will 'come out'.

RAGAN (23): Yugoslavian, could speak English only with a Slavic accent, and had a drooping moustache. Read Serbo-Croatian, did drawings, was a karate and munitions expert with a criminal record. He was a communist and an atheist. His role was to protect the others, and he was predominant when there was danger.

ALLEN (18): the only right-handed alter, smoked cigarettes and parted his hair on the side. Played the drums and was a manipulative con man.

TOMMY (16): played the saxophone, painted and was knowledgeable about electronics. Generally antisocial. An escapologist who demonstrated his ability to escape from straitjackets while on remand.

CHRISTENE (3): an English girl who drew butterflies and flowers.

ADALANA (19): a shy lesbian who wrote poetry and liked cooking and housework.

DAVID (8): small, highly sensitive. His job was to absorb all the pain felt by the others.

Some of these personalities consented to take IQ tests, making it possible to compare their scores. These ranged from 69 (David) to 120 (Allen). Milligan claimed to have been abused as a child by his stepfather, who threatened to bury him alive if he talked about it to anyone else. As a demonstration, he was buried with a pipe over his face for air. At one stage of the trial, his brother was able to partially corroborate the allegations of abuse.

Pre-trial treatment was given for a period of 3 months to partially fuse the personalities, so that he would be fit to stand trial. He was in fact found not guilty of rape and kidnapping by reason of insanity, though many who had contact with him thought that he was just a liar. He was admitted to a psychiatric unit, and eventually released in 1988 with his personality allegedly fused. Subsequently, he was arrested for another crime (not sexual), but there was no claim of MPD.

Evaluation

The importance of Milligan's case lies in the fact that not only does it raise the issue of the legal implications of MPD; it also provides a good example of the relatively rare male multiple. According to Putnam et al. (1986), and Ross et al. (1989), 90% of diagnosed multiples are female. Hacking (1995) offers four explanations for this:

- Male multiples are more likely than females to commit crimes and therefore end up in the criminal justice system rather than the psychiatric system.
- Dissociation is a more culturally acceptable way for women to express their distress than it is for men.
- MPD is the result of child abuse, especially sexual, and women are more likely to suffer from this than men.

89

- Women are more suggestible than men, and therefore more open to suggestions made by therapists.

In terms of the legal implications, Milligan was the first person in America to be acquitted of a major crime because of an insanity plea based on MPD. Initially considered a neurosis, rather than a psychosis, MPD had not previously been regarded as severe enough to warrant a judgement of insanity being made. Since then there have been other such cases. Coons (1991) reported that there had been 19 cases in America from 1977 to 1991. Of these, two were found not guilty by reason of insanity, two were incompetent to stand trial and one was found guilty but mentally ill. Slovenko (1993) reported a case of murder in which the defendant claimed the crime had been committed by her 9-year-old alter. MPD has also been used as the basis of successful insanity pleas in forgery cases (Allison 1978). In England and Wales, MPD has not been used as a defence in court to date, although case studies have been reported in legal journals, as Box 3.3 demonstrates.

BOX 3.3 MPD and the courts (James & Schramm 1998)

A case was reported of a 33-year-old American arrested for stealing antiques when visiting Britain. Four personalities were detected: K, a cool antiques thief; D, an obsessive-compulsive character; R, a 7-year-old child; and another irritable adult. The man satisfied the criteria for MPD, but also for obsessive-compulsive disorder, borderline personality disorder and antisocial personality disorder. He was advised to plead guilty in the light of the weight of evidence against him, given a suspended sentence and allowed to leave the country. At the time of the trial, the 7-year-old was in charge. That caused legal problems because he would then be a minor, below the age of criminal responsibility, as well as being too young to instruct a solicitor. It was considered that he was fit to plead when in the adult state, but there was concern that in court he might revert to the child, leading to a plea of unfit to plead not guilty by reason of insanity.

According to Lewis and Bard (1991), there are four major defences that can be presented in MPD cases:

- The individual has no control over the secondary personalities, and is therefore not responsible for them.
- The individual cannot remember what the alters did, and therefore cannot defend them.
- The individual does not know right from wrong because of suffering from MPD.
- The individual is not accountable because she or he is unconscious of the alters' behaviours.

Alters, however, pose considerable legal problems. For example, it is not clear what would happen if, in America, a child alter were to take over from someone facing the death penalty. (Slovenko 1989 reported that there were 10 females with MPD on death row, so this is not an impossible situation.)

Another problem is that until the primary personality is established, each alter should have separate representation (French & Schechmeister 1983). The courts have also recognised alters as being separate for testimony purposes (Perr 1991). Saks (1994) reported a case where 6 of the supposed 47 alters of a female witness were sworn in separately. Sarah alleged that two of her personalities had been raped by a man who had sex with one of her other alters. When she switched personalitites, she had to retake the oath. The man was found guilty of second degree sexual assault because he knowingly had intercourse with someone suffering from mental disorder that made her unable to appraise her conduct. In theory, one alter could presumably be called on to give testimony against another, if they are all treated as responsible for their own behaviour. It is difficult to see how this can be sustained, however, as they do not have an independent existence. Dawson (1999) argues that in law, the person who carries out an act is considered to be the agent of the whole person, and that person is responsible for the act. Therefore, the insanity defence is inappropriate in this instance, since legally, if not psychologically, the person is still a single entity.

Progress exercise

Considering these cases, and any others with which you are familiar, note down any similarities and differences that you can think of between the symptoms of MPD and those of:

(a) schizophrenia,

(b) depression,

(c) antisocial personality disorder.

(You may have to refer back to Chapter 2 for details of these, and case studies.)

Origins of MPD

Five major theories exist about the origins of MPD; you will see that they are broadly derived from the different models of mental disorder outlined in Chapter 1.

The biological approach

The finding in the case of Eve that there were physiological differences between the personalities suggests that there may be a biological basis for the disorder. Note, however, that any observed differences may be the cause or the effect of the problems. Putnam (1984) measured the Visual Evoked Potentials (records of activity in the cortex) of the alters of MPD patients and compared them with controls who were asked to simulate alters. The real alters showed more variability than the simulated alters, indicating physiological differences. This study could also be used to support the argument that the condition is real, rather than faked.

Tsai et al. (1999) carried out a study of a 47-year-old woman patient called Marnie, using **fMRI** scanners to observe what happened in the brain when she switched personalities. They found that the **hippocampus**, an area of the brain involved in memory, was shrunken to about half the normal size. This feature has been documented before, in other cases of people who have suffered repeated trauma (such as PTSD and child abuse cases). Changes in hippocampal and temporal lobe function were also observed during the switching process. Since the hippocampus seems to be the brain's centre for 'printing' memories, and memories could be regarded as crucial to our sense of self (our knowledge of our own personality), such damage could well lead to, or be associated with, the observed problems.

The psychodynamic approach

Janet (1859–1947) was the first to claim that what he called double consciousness was caused by childhood trauma that had become buried in the unconscious. His theory was that the mind is made up of 'psychological automatisms', which are clusters of perceptions and thoughts that are available to conscious awareness. Following an unbearable trauma, one or more of these may become split off or dissociated, so that it is no longer under the control of the conscious mind.

According to later psychodynamic views, MPD is regarded as an extreme case of the use of repression as an ego defence mechanism. Painful memories – or, in this case, entire identities – are repressed from consciousness (Putnam 1989). Where childhood involved extreme trauma, such as the abuse suffered by Sybil, the memory for the abuse may be more effectively repressed if the entire personality that experienced it is also repressed. The child imagines that the abuse is happening to another 'self'. The primary personality is typically very inhibited, which supports this idea.

More recent formulations of this idea (e.g. Davies & Frawley 1991) have postulated a **trauma-dissociation model** of MPD. This has taken up Janet's original concept of dissociation and linked it with Hilgard's (1977) neo-dissociation theory of hypnosis. Hilgard argued that during hypnosis, some cognitive systems can be separated off from consciousness by an amnestic barrier, so that two dissociated streams of thought can exist alongside one another. In this model, then, a child who is so constitutionally predisposed can split off (or dissociate) painful memories from consciousness as a protective device. These then become the alter, separated from consciousness by an amnestic barrier.

Evidence for this explanation can be derived from the child abuse reported in many cases. However, not all cases do report abuse, and not all cases of abuse develop MPD (Bliss 1980). It is also difficult to explain why the reports of abuse appeared to increase in cases reported after 1980, compared to those reported prior to that date (Goff & Sims

1993). The prevalence in different countries does not fit well with this explanation, either, since the countries where it is most common are not those where trauma might be most common; compare trauma-ridden Africa with peaceful Canada, for example. It has also been reported (Mair 1997) that the recovery of such memories does not appear to be associated with therapeutic gain, as the psychodynamic theorists would expect.

Self-hypnosis approach

In this view, MPD is a form of self-hypnosis used by sufferers to help them to forget unpleasant events (Bliss 1986). They are able to separate themselves mentally from both their bodies and their surroundings. In support of this idea, MPD is considered to begin around 4–6 years of age, which is when children are at their most susceptible to hypnotic suggestion (Kluft 1987). Further support can be derived from the finding that most MPD patients appear to be highly suggestible. Sybil, for example, was reported to be able to enter a trance spontaneously.

The behavioural approach

The focus here is also on the traumatic experiences associated with MPD. The difference is that according to this view forgetting is seen as a rewarding experience because it reduces anxiety. According to operant conditioning theory, it will therefore become a learned response, because of its reinforcing properties.

Another theory based on learning principles is that of **state-dependent learning**. It has repeatedly been shown that information that is learned while in one state (e.g. mood) is best recalled when the individual is in the same state (Eich 1995). MPD sufferers may simply have very selective memories, which means that their recall will depend on them being in exactly the same physiological state when recalling as when the memories were laid down (Putnam 1992).

Socio-cultural approach

According to this view, some features of our culture may promote MPD. For example, Varma et al. (1981) point out that modern Western culture has placed an emphasis on role playing, particularly through the entertainment industry. Some theories of hypnosis (Spanos et al. 1985) see hypnosis as a state of role enactment in which imagination and suggestibility play a key part, so this could link up with the previous explanation. The fact that there is considerable cultural variation in prevalence and that 90% of cases are women (see previous sections) could also fit in with this explanation. The socio-cultural explanations of MPD, whether emphasising spontaneous or iatrogenic origins for the disorder, have been evaluated in the first section of this chapter

MPD and child abuse

Here we will concentrate on the major theoretical explanation for MPD, the trauma-dissociation model that links predisposition with a history of abuse. Behavioural and self-hypnosis explanations also depend on the existence of previous trauma or abuse, so the investigation of such patients for memories of abuse is a key issue. Has research confirmed that abuse is commonplace during the childhood of MPD sufferers? The reliability and validity of the evidence on this issue depends crucially on the methods used to obtain the information; this in turn depends on the techniques used in the course of therapy, so we must consider these next.

Treatment

The first true multiple, Louis Vivet, was subjected to a wide variety of strange treatments, including the application of magnets to his body, morphine and emetics. The presence of gold bromide was found to be capable of inducing a personality change. There were only two things that could halt an attack of hysterical symptoms: one was pressure on either the Achilles tendon or the tendon below the kneecap; the other was having his testicles tightly squeezed by his doctors. Treatment has moved on since those days, but given the lack of knowledge about origins of the disorder, it is no less speculative.

Spontaneous recovery is rare (Spiegel 1994) and treatment often includes the administration of anti-anxiety or antidepressant drugs initially. Psychotherapy usually involves three processes:

- *Recognising the disorder* This is largely an educational exercise for both patients and their families. Videotapes may be shown of other cases of MPD, and of the alters, and hypnosis may be used to make the sub-personalities aware of one another (Allen 1993). The patient may be asked if she or he ever feels that there is another part of the personality they wish to reveal. Once out, this alter will be named.

- *Recovering memories* Using psychodynamic therapy, hypnosis or drugs, the aim is to help the patients to recall their missing memories. At this stage, they may become aggressive towards themselves and others (Kelly 1993). Re-enactments called abreactions are used to get the alters to reveal their memories. These can go on for as long as 9 hours (Braun 1990) although about 3 hours is typical (Putnam et al. 1986). Guided imagery or visualisation may also be used, in which the patient is talked through an imaginary scene to help to awaken memories. 'Screen techniques' involve the visualisation of a cinema screen on which abuse or other memories are being replayed. Another technique is the use of 'journaling' – keeping a journal to help pick out recurrent thoughts.

- *Integrating sub-personalities into one* Again a range of approaches can be used, such as assertiveness training for the primary personality, or group discussions between the sub-personalities. Coping skills need to be consolidated to reduce the risk of future dissociation. Psychodynamic therapists may concentrate on the achievement of insight, so that the patient can deal with the memories in a more constructive way than by dissociation in the future.

Progress exercise

Before you read on, consider carefully whether any of the techniques outlined above, used to help patients recognise the disorder and recover memories, may be conducive to the development of MPD as an iatrogenic disorder. Could they make the patient more susceptible to influence from the therapist?

There are three questions to ask about the treatment of MPD:

- Does the treatment work? If it does, this would go some way towards supporting the trauma model.

- Are there generally recovered memories of child abuse? If there are, again the trauma model has some support.
- Are the memories accurate? This must be established as well, before the model can be accepted.

Does the treatment work?

The relatively small number of cases reported means that it is difficult to assess the effectiveness of these treatments. Most case studies that are reported indicate that integration can be achieved, but we have already seen that many of these cases are suspect for one reason or another, and that problems of various sorts do persist after treatment has been terminated. Ross (1989) has argued that 75% of patients can be treated to integration in less than 2½ years, but there is no evidence to support this claim.

Mair (1997) has argued that therapy may do more harm than good. Taking into account initial variations in severity, she found an inverse relationship between future well-being and number of treatment sessions received – with more treatment being associated with worse outcomes. She also notes that none of her sample showed 'overall evidence of benefit', especially since there were serious risks attached to the treatment. The risks she referred to included self-harm, suicide attempts, and horrific new (recovered) memories that had seriously disrupted family relationships in many cases.

How frequent are recovered memories of child abuse?

Are there in fact reports of child abuse in a significant number of patients seen? Since most MPD cases are female, and more females than males suffer abuse (Bentovim & Tranter 1994, for example, reported a ratio of 4:1), it may be expected that there would be. Taylor and Martin (1944) found no allegations of abuse in any of the cases they looked at prior to that date. Since then, however, most patients do claim to have suffered abuse. Early surveys (e.g. Putnam et al. 1986) showed that 83% reported sexual abuse, but these have not been objectively verified. According to Ross et al. (1991), in a study of 100 patients, 95.1% had a history of abuse. A review of the literature showed that 68–86% reported child or adolescent sexual abuse, and 60–82% physical abuse. A significant number, then, do report abuse.

Are the recovered memories accurate?

The next question is whether those reports are accurate. Freud himself was very sceptical about the abuse reported by his patients, and eventually decided that the reports were sexual fantasies. This led him to abandon his seduction theory. His critics (e.g. Masson 1988) have rejected this view and have produced evidence that the memories may have been genuine. In many modern cases it has been suggested that the memories are elicited from patients during the course of treatment procedures that may not produce reliable memories. Simpson (1995) considers that the examination methods used by therapists resemble interrogation techniques. The use of powerful drugs, as in the case of Sybil, leading questions and hypnosis have all been criticised. For example, Acocella (1999) has noted that high doses of benzodiazepines may be given to combat anxiety, since MPD patients are considered to be resistant to their effects. Ross (1995) admitted in a court case that the patient concerned had been given a dose that was 100 times the maximum.

Leading questions that have been shown by Loftus (1993) to be in common use include 'has anything like that ever happened to you?'. Sanders et al. (1999) found that mere exposure to stories about the childhood experiences of others altered the memories of participants in experiments, leading many to report that the events had actually happened to them. Guided imagery can also be used to make direct suggestions to patients, and hypnotic recall may also be susceptible to suggestion.

The use of hypnosis

Hypnotic recall has been regarded with suspicion for some time. McDougall (1938), commenting on the case of Miss Beauchamp (studied by Morton Prince in 1906), noted that the use of hypnosis 'may have moulded the course of its development to a degree that cannot be determined'. The American Medical Association in 1985 stated that 'recollections obtained during hypnosis . . . appear to be less reliable than nonhypnotic recall' (Acocella 1999, p. 13). This is because patients can be cued more easily by the therapist, and because their confidence in the memories produced is increased (without justification). Kline (1952) has noted that if the appropriate suggestion is made, patients can be made to recall former lives as chimps, for example. According to Laurence et al. (1998), 'hypnosis increases productivity rather than accuracy of recall – this productivity is not real but guided by the verbal and nonverbal cues of the recall setting' (p. 330). On the other hand, Kluft (1998) argues that provided it is not accompanied by leading questions, hypnosis is useful. He found that memories recovered during hypnosis are often able to be confirmed by independent sources.

Independent verification

What is needed is independent corroboration of the reports to decide if this is in fact the case. In 1991, Hornstein and Tyson reported that 61/66 cases they investigated had reported independently documentable trauma. Coons (1986) found corroborated abuse in 17/20 patients, although in some cases the abuse was simply spanking. In 1994 Coons found corroborated abuse histories in 21/22 patients, and Kluft (1995) found that 56% of abuse memories were corroborated in his sample of 34 carefully screened patients. He accepted the corroboration only if it involved a witness (usually a sibling) or a confession from the perpetrator (usually a parent or sibling). Lewis et al. (1997) found objective evidence of severe abuse and early dissociation in a study of 12 murderers suffering from MPD. The murderers themselves had partial or total amnesia for the abuse, but it was reported by others. Clearly then, some, but not all, reports of abuse can be confirmed independently.

False memory syndrome

Despite this, there is sufficient concern about the reliability of these reports for the term **'false memory syndrome'** to have been coined. This refers to 'a condition in which a person's identity and interpersonal relationships are centred around a memory of traumatic experience which is objectively false but which the person strongly believes' (Kihlstrom 1995). The False Memory Syndrome Foundation has been set up to defend accused parents, and the British Psychological Society (2000) has issued a set of guidelines for practitioners working with clients in situations where recovered memories may arise. These guidelines are shown in Box 3.4. In America, insurance companies now issue policies for therapists containing a clause that voids the cover if hypnosis is used to obtain memories of child abuse (Acocella 1999). This is because legal proceedings for negligence, malpractice and insurance fraud have become commonplace; therapists usually lose the case, and claims of up to 10.6 million dollars have been awarded against them. Thus the reliability of these reports is not generally considered to be high.

BOX 3.4 Guidelines for psychologists working with clients in contexts in which issues related to recovered memories may arise

Preamble

The following guidelines are intended to apply to psychologists working in all professional contexts in which such issues may arise. It is clearly part of the professional duty of such psychologists to seek to maintain an awareness of this debate and to develop an empirical and professional perspective on false memory/recovered memories, and base their practice on sound psychological principles and evidence as a counter-balance to the polarised beliefs that abound in this emotive area.

As the result of extensive review by the Society and other bodies there can be no doubt for psychologists of the existence of child sexual abuse (CSA) as a serious social and individual problem commonly with long-lasting effects. In addition there can be little doubt that at least some recovered memories of CSA are recollections of historical events. However, there is genuine cause for concern that some interventions can lead clients to develop illusory memories or may foster false beliefs concerning CSA.

Members seeking discussion of terms and background material on these issues are referred to the Society's earlier document *Recovered Memories: Report of the BPS Working Party* (The British Psychological Society 1995b).

Guidelines

1 The welfare and interests of clients are the primary concern of psycho-logists working with them. This concern includes the requirement to maintain respect for the client's autonomy and confidentiality the extent of which should ideally be clarified and agreed at the outset of the professional engagement.

---

2 It may be necessary for psychologists in caring, assessment and therapeutic roles to be open to the emergence of memories of trauma which were not previously available to the client's awareness.

3 It is important always to take the client who recovers memories seriously. The first response of the psychologist should be to accept that what the client tells them reflects their reality and respect their feelings. Nevertheless the psychologist should avoid drawing premature conclusions about the historical truth of a recovered memory.

4 Psychologists must be aware that the question of whether traumatic memory is processed, stored and recalled differently from normal memory is currently unresolved. Unusual, dramatic, powerful or vivid memories, and 'flashback' bodily sensations cannot be relied upon as evidence of the historical truth or falsity of the recovered memories.

5 Psychologists need to tolerate, and help their client tolerate, uncertainty and ambiguity regarding the clients early experience as eventually they may both have to accept that the historical truth cannot be known, and that helping the client to make reasonable sense of their lives is not the same as discovering objective facts.

6 Psychologists should be alert to a range of possibilities; for example that a recovered memory may be literally/historically true or false, or may be partly true, thematically true or metaphorically true, or may derive from fantasy or dream material. Discovering that some aspects of a 'memory' are displaced, metaphorical, or part of a construction or narrative derived from the therapeutic relationship should not lead psychologists to immediately discount the rest of that memory. Likewise, the discovery that some aspects of a memory are factually accurate does not imply that the whole content of the memory is factual. It is not really possible to establish whether a memory represents factual events without external corroboration.

7 Whilst it may be part of a psychologist's work to help clients to think about their early experiences they should avoid imposing their own conclusions about what took place in childhood.

8 Child sexual abuse should not be deduced on the basis of presenting symptoms such as eating disorders alone. There is a high probability of false positives in such deductions as there are other possible explanations for psychological problems. The construction of syndromes and the use of symptom check-lists in diagnosis in relation to past sexual abuse are currently available.

9 Psychologists should avoid being drawn into a search for memories of abuse, as abused clients (and non-abused clients who are psychologically disturbed) are vulnerable and may be traumatised or overwhelmed by material that has not arisen spontaneously in the course of their psychological work. Psychologists should avoid engaging in activities and techniques which are intended to reveal indications of past sexual abuse of which the client has no memory. When psychologists use such techniques (e.g. hypnosis) for other purposes they must be aware that these techniques may make memory more confident but less reliable.

10 Psychologists must be alert to the dangers of suggestion. Potential sources of suggestion include subtle cues about the psychologist's attitudes and beliefs that may be inferred from the therapeutic context (e.g. particular books on the shelf) or client contact with 'survivor literature' and subcultures of abuse. Psychologists must be aware that there may be situations in which clients are motivated to recall memories of abuse for a variety of ends.

11 Psychologists working therapeutically must be aware of their inevitable engagement in the client's narrative. Whilst taking care about the implications of active investigation and suggestion, they should not seek to manage these risks simply by refusing to deal with past events and 'work in the present', since this actively denies the client's experience and is unlikely to meet their needs.

12 Psychologists working therapeutically should be aware of the likely impact of their work on their clients' families and wider social network and should not rule out renegotiating the contract with their clients to enable them to meet with relevant family members. However the boundaries of a client's autonomy and confidentiality should only be breached in rare circumstances, ideally as agreed at the outset of the professional engagement.

13 Psychologists should be clear about the circumstances in which they would feel ethically or legally obliged to breach confidentiality. They should carefully assess the risk of self-harm and the risk of abuse to minors. Psychologists working in the public services should be aware of their child protection guidelines and procedures and abide by them. Psychologists working independently should also be aware of their ethical responsibilities to protect others from significant harm.

14 If the role of the psychologist is to obtain evidence that is reliable in forensic terms, they need to restrict themselves to procedures that enhance reliability and avoid techniques which are known to reduce reliability, such as hypnosis or suggestion and leading questions. The same care should be taken whenever action (e.g. informing other agencies, legal action, family confrontation) outside the consulting room is being considered.

15 The psychologist has a responsibility to help the client to consider carefully any action to be taken outside the consulting room. The client may wish to take independent legal advice with a view to prosecution of or litigation against an alleged abuser. It is inappropriate to make the continuation of treatment/consultation contingent on such decisions/ actions. Psychologists must be prepared to accept that it may not be the client's choice to deal with these matters therapeutically or through family confrontation or legal process.

16 Psychologists are reminded of their guidelines for good practice. These may be particularly important when working with clients who disclose memories of childhood abuse. The guidelines will include sections on keeping and preserving appropriate records and seeking appropriate consultation and supervision.

References

British Psychological Society, The (1995a). *Division of Clinical Psychology: Professional Practice Guidelines*. Leicester: The British Psychological Society.

British Psychological Society, The (1995b). *Recovered Memories: Report of the BPS Working Party*. Leicester: The British Psychological Society.

British Psychological Society, The (1998). *Guidelines for the Professional Practice of Counselling Psychology*. Leicester: The British Psychological Society.

Brandon, S. (1998). Recovered memory debate [Letter to the editor]. *The Psychologist*, *11*, 465.

Brandon, S., Boakes, J., Glaser, D., & Green, R. (1998). Recovered memories of childhood sexual abuse: Implications for clinical practice. *British Journal of Psychiatry*, *172*, 293–307.

Farrants, J. R. (1998). The 'false memory' debate: A critical review of the research on recovered memories of child sexual abuse. *Counselling Psychology Quarterly*, *11*, 229–238.

Fox, J. (1998). Recovered memory debate [Letter to the editor]. *The Psychologist*, *11*, 466–467.

Mollon, P. (1998). *Remembering trauma: A psychotherapist's guide to memory and illusion*. Appendix: Guidelines for psychoanalytically orientated psychotherapists for the avoidance of generating or colluding with false memories. Chichester: Wiley.

Mollon, P. (2000). [Review of the book *Memory, Trauma Treatment and the Law*]. *Clinical Psychology Forum*, *136*, 42–43.

Morton, J. (1998a). Royal College fall-out. *The Psychologist*, *11*, 408.

Morton, J. (1998b). Recovered memory debate [Invited reply to letters to the editor]. *The Psychologist*, *11*, 467.

Morton, J., Lunt, I., Mollon, P., Taylor, M., Lindsay, D. S., Skinner, A., Frankish, P., Cullen, C., & Fonagy, P. (1996). *BPS Professional Affairs Board Symposium on Recovered Memories*. Leicester: The British Psychological Society.

Ost, J. (1998). Recovered memory debate [Letter to the editor]. *The Psychologist*, *11*, 467.

Weiskrantz, L. (1998). Recovered memory debate [Letter to the editor]. *The Psychologist*, *11*, 465–466.

First published in *The Psychologist*, 13, 5

Does childhood abuse lead to adult disorder?

The next question is whether childhood abuse does relate to adult disorder (MPD in particular). Schacter et al. (1989) compared the frequency of autobiographical memories in an MPD patient with those of a control group. They found that the patient was unable to recall personal events before the age of 10 years, and her memory was poor for events that occurred when she was 10–12 years old, suggesting that repression may occur. Allison (1978) reported that the first personality split occurs in 45% of cases before the age of 5 years, and 85% occur before the age of 10, which again suggests some sort of childhood problem. Sanders and Giolas (1991), looking at adolescent psychiatric patients, found a correlation between abuse and family discord and dissociative experiences. In the normal population, dissociative symptoms have been shown to have increased after the traumatic experience of the San Francisco earthquake of 1989 (Cardena & Speigel 1993).

MPD, however, seems to be only one possible outcome; a history of abuse has also been reported in prostitutes, child molesters and eating disorder, depression, suicide and substance abuse cases (Walker et al. 1988). A recent British text on child abuse and its consequences does not mention MPD at all (Corby 2000). MPD is also less common in black ethnic groups, despite the finding that the rate of abuse in such groups is double that in the white populace (US Department of Health & Human Services 1996). Putnam (1997) found that if families were matched on all criteria except for sexual abuse, there was no difference in the levels of adult psychological disorder shown. Emotional neglect was found to be much more damaging. Long-term effects are more likely when the abuse involves violence, is penetrative and of longer duration (Ussher & Dewberry 1995). The most likely long-term effect is poor sexual adjustment (Knutson 1995). Trauma related to disclosure can also lead to subsequent mental disorder (Spaccarelli 1994). Overall, the evidence for a specific link is not strong.

Are traumatic memories repressed?

Another line of research relates to whether such traumatic memories are in fact repressed. From a review of the literature, Kendall-Tackett et al. (1993) conclude that 'amnesia is a rare consequence of childhood abuse in children'. Williams (1994) followed up a sample of 129 females treated for abuse at the ages of 10 months to 12 years. When they were adult, 88% remembered being abused as children, indicating that repression is not the norm. Laurence et al. (1998) conclude that 'There is at the moment no scientific evidence to support a mental process akin to repression and/or dissociation at play in childhood abuse' (p. 332).

Conclusion

It would appear that the treatment may not be very helpful (at best), that abuse may be reported in a significant number of cases, some of which are probably accurate, and that abuse has only weak links with

MPD and later repression of memories. Thus there is not a great deal of support for the trauma model. However, this still leaves us with a question – why are there so many reports of abuse in these patients?

Evaluation: spontaneous or iatrogenic?

The term 'iatrogenic', when applied to a disorder, means that it is induced in the patient by the words or actions of the clinician. In this context, the suggestion is that if clinicians are on the lookout for the disorder, they may make suggestions or interpretations to patients (particularly under hypnosis) that could cue the behaviours they are expecting, i.e. dissociation or reports of abuse (Frick 1995). This can be contrasted with a spontaneously occurring disorder which has not been influenced by the clinician. We have looked at some of the evidence pertaining to this debate in earlier sections of the chapter, and also introduced the idea of social constructionism as an alternative explanation. It is suggested here that the high rate of abuse reports in MPD patients may be the result of this type of social process.

Trends in prevalence

There are clear parallels between the rise in reported cases of child abuse and the rise in cases of MPD (Apter 1991), which could support the argument about child abuse being causative. However, as stated earlier, not all cases have suffered abuse, and not all abused children dissociate. It is also possible that both child abuse and MPD are on the increase, not as a result of genuine increases in rate of occurrence, but as a result of media publicity and reduced inhibitions about reporting such problems. Both MPD and reports of abuse could be attributed to overzealous clinicians. Hacking (1995) comments 'Psychiatry did not discover that . . . child abuse causes multiple personality. It forged that connection' (Acocella 1999, p. 72).

Social changes

In an earlier section, we discussed developments in psychology that might have paved the way for the observed increases in MPD in recent decades. Other developments in society may have forged the link with child abuse; these are the child protection movement and the feminist movement.

In 1962, Kempe et al. publicised what they referred to as 'battered child syndrome', which led to legislation to protect children and an increase in public awareness of abuse. Claims of child abuse rose by 900% between 1976 and 1986 in some areas of America. Some of this increase may have been due to changes in definitions of abuse. Wyatt (1985) reported a 62% increase in Los Angeles, when the definition of abuse included unwanted sexual remarks. Peters (1986) reported a figure of 6% when it was restricted to forced sexual contact before the age of 18 years. The increase in divorce, which tripled in the 1960s and 1970s, may also have been implicated. Absent fathers are easier to accuse, and stepfathers may be more likely to abuse (Daly & Wilson 1994).

Feminists identified with the finding that most abuse was directed at female children, and sought help from assorted 'recovery manuals' published at the time to try and find their own memories of abuse. Bass and Davis (1988), for example, published a best-selling book called *The courage to heal* that was implicated in almost all of the several hundred cases of accused families reviewed by Wakefield and Underwager (1992). This book contained a checklist of over 900 symptoms (including 'Do you ever feel different to other people') that were considered to be indicators of abuse. Detection of abuse also involved attending 'survivor groups' with the view that hearing the memories of others could lead to one's own memories emerging (a process known as '**chaining**'). Reinforcement in the form of attention would be given for those who 'conquered their denial'.

The mass media

The mass media involved celebrities such as Oprah Winfrey in the proceedings, and accusations escalated to include **satanic ritual abuse** (SRA) involving the skinning and eating of live babies. One television station in America even screened a series about detecting satanic cults in your home town, between 1988 and 1990 (Acocella 1999). MPD patients began to claim that their alters had been specifically created by satanists to carry out specific evil tasks. In 1995 the FBI stated that they had been unable to corroborate any of the reports of satanism. If

MPD patients are in fact highly suggestible, as has been claimed, such media reports may provide a form of training for their role. Ganaway (1989) in fact reported that following the SRA panic alters became progressively more odd, including cases involving a lobster and a unicorn. Little wonder that Mair (1999) states 'they seem to be like chameleons, reflecting the preoccupations of the age' (p. 79).

According to Acocella (1999) it may also be the case that the diagnosis of MPD may appeal to clients. It provides an explanation for their current, apparently groundless unhappiness that places the responsibility firmly on what others have done in the past. A possibility of cure is also given, and for many who have had previous diagnoses and treatments that have failed, this is appealing. It also provides solidarity, via the feminist movement, with other sufferers. Political problems, such as the abuse of children and oppression of women, are thereby transformed into medical problems, and defused.

Another negative consequence of such publicity is that, like pornography, the recovery literature may provide publicity, propagating the very behaviours it decries. Acocella's conclusion is that cultural changes can be considered to be responsible for both acknowledging and encouraging MPD. Thus: 'the social construction of mental illness – the fact that the forms mental illness takes (indeed the very notion that there is such a thing as mental illness) are the product of shifting cultural assumptions – must be taken into account to explain the rise of MPD' (p. 28).

Conclusion

The important question, perhaps, is whether it helps to view MPD in one way, as iatrogenic, or the other, as spontaneous. To quote Mersky (1992, cited in Hacking 1995, p. 16) 'The diagnosis of MPD represents a misdirection of effort that hinders the resolution of serious psychological problems in the lives of the patients.' From another angle, Spiegel (1993, cited in Hacking 1995, p. 18) has argued that 'the problem is not having more than one personality; it is having less than one personality.' Hacking (1995) looks at the consequences of the way that society currently responds to such individuals in order to decide the issue. His conclusion is that what is being done is wrong at the moral level, in the sense that it gives those concerned what he refers to as a false consciousness. The consciousness produced by therapy is false because it fails to provide an adequate explanation for the problems experienced, yet encourages clients to believe that those problems have been solved; and 'false consciousness is contrary to the growth and maturing of a person who knows herself. It is contrary to what the philosophers call freedom' (p. 267).

With this in mind, those involved in the MPD movement have had to change their approach to the problem. In 1989, Ross argued that it was not an iatrogenic artefact; in 1997 he conceded that it was not *solely* iatrogenic. The number of new diagnoses is now falling, the treatment offered nowadays places less emphasis on hypnosis and past traumas, and more on building ego strength. Half of the treatment centres in America have closed in the last 5 years (Acocella 1999).

Chapter summary

In this chapter we have looked at the nature of MPD, the diagnostic criteria, and how it may be measured. The prevalence of the disorder in different periods of history and in different countries has been used to introduce the debate about whether it is a spontaneous disorder, iatrogenic, or socially constructed. The case studies of Eve, Sybil and Billy Milligan have been described and evaluated in terms of the accuracy of reporting, influence of the therapist, gender and legal implications. Theories about the origins of the disorder have been described and evaluated; the trauma model has been investigated in detail, and it has been concluded that although links with trauma are weak, significant numbers of patients have reported childhood abuse. This has been analysed in the light of social conditions prevailing at the time, and it has been concluded that the social construction of MPD has not been helpful to patients.

Summarise in table form the arguments for MPD as spontaneous, iatrogenic and socially constructed. You will need to look at all sections of the chapter to select material to back up your points.

Review exercise

Further reading

Acocella, J. (1999) *Creating Hysteria: Women and Multiple Personality Disorder*. San Francisco: Jossey Bass. (Very involving read – she is a journalist as well as a psychologist – with a wealth of detail and interesting reports of research.)

Lynn, S. & McConkey, K. (1998). *Truth in Memory*. New York: Guilford. (Several interesting articles on the accuracy of memory in abuse cases.)

Hacking, I. (1995) *Rewriting the Soul: Multiple Personality and the Sciences of Memory*. New Jersey: Princeton University Press. (Historical analysis of the disorder, extremely well written but quite demanding.)

4

Cultural and subcultural issues in abnormality

 The relevance of culture and subculture
How culture defines what is normal and abnormal
Differences in prevalence of mental disorders
Culture-bound syndromes
Differential treatment according to culture

The relevance of culture and subculture

Some definitions

The term '**culture**' refers to 'a learned system of values, beliefs, meanings, rules and practices that are passed from one generation to the next in patterned ways. Culture provides a way of looking at the world and of experiencing it' (Flaskerud 2000). As such, it will affect beliefs, values, attitudes, ideologies, rules, practices (such as child-rearing, for example), language, family systems, social structures, art, technology and artefacts – in short, ways of thinking and ways of living.

Two other terms are often confused with culture (although they are not equivalent), and will therefore be clarified here. '**Race**' implies membership of a group that is distinct biologically or genetically from other groups. This term is rarely considered appropriate nowadays, since many groups in society are biologically diverse, and genetic differences within apparent racial groups are often greater than those between them. The preferred term is '**ethnicity**', a subjective term referring to the sense of belonging to a particular group, which may be based on race, religion or culture.

Subculture is a subdivision within a cultural group, which shares distinctive behaviours, beliefs and attitudes. In this chapter we will be exploring the implications of cultural and subcultural differences by looking at mental disorder in different ethnic and national groups, and at differences associated with gender, age and social class.

Relevance

Anthropologists refer to the organised bodies of knowledge passed on to individuals by their culture as **cultural meaning systems**. According to Castillo (1997, p. 20) 'a cultural meaning system generally structures cognitive reality for an entire society'. These meaning systems serve four functions, as follows:

- *Representational function* They provide systems for symbolically representing the world and for communication between individuals. Language (written and spoken) and art are examples.
- *Constructive function* Through communication, cultural entities are created. These are socially agreed rituals, explanations or ways of doing things; examples are marriage, property and the family. The diagnostic categories used in DSM can be seen as cultural entities, in the sense that they are arrived at through the consensus of a committee of experts, and then by general social agreement they are applied universally and become reality for all those involved.
- *Directive function* The cultural entities created through group consensus then have an effect on the way that people in that culture (and sometimes outside, as we shall see) live their lives. A particular diagnosis will affect the individual concerned (e.g. an elderly person diagnosed with the beginnings of Alzheimer's disease will undoubt-edly be distraught), will evoke a response from others (which may be positive and helpful or negative and stigmatising), and may lead the clinician to apply a particular form of treatment.
- *Evocative function* The cultural meaning system also provides rules about how to feel. Thus in Western culture generally, losing your job or failing an exam would be regarded as cause for feeling unhappy, but only for a prescribed period of time.

Cultural differences in behaviour

Differences in cultural and subcultural backgrounds can therefore be seen as having a profound influence on all aspects of life, including our views about what is normal, expected behaviour and what is not. For example, in some cultures (such as the Mediterranean) the expression of emotions is valued and encouraged, whereas in others (such as the English and Chinese) it is frowned on and considered inappropriate behaviour. There is also considerable variation in the emphasis on an **individualist** versus **collectivist** outlook. In Western individualist cultures the emphasis is on the self, achievement of personal happiness and status. In collectivist cultures, the family and community come first, and everything the individual does is for their benefit rather than for himself. He must avoid bringing shame on them at all costs.

Cultures have a range of **social norms** that specify appropriate behaviours for different groups of persons in that culture. Behaviour outside those norms may be acceptable if it forms part of a '**rite of reversal**' (such as a carnival), i.e. it takes place in a specified setting. Communing with the ancestors and hearing their voices would be acceptable in North American Indian culture; entering trance states or other altered states of consciousness is acceptable, or even desirable, in many cultures, given the right context. White, Western cultures, however, have a strong emphasis on the existence of objective reality, and regard hearing voices as abnormal behaviour. In some cultures, treatment involves religious and spiritual practices; in others, it would be visiting a clinician (although some would still see this as a disgrace).

Culture and mental disorder

Given these differences, the aim of **transcultural psychiatry** (a discipline that has sprung up to link the fields of psychiatry and anthropology) has been to look at the nature of mental disorder in other cultures. If abnormal behaviour is culture-free, and biologically determined, then it should take exactly the same form in all cultures, known as **absolutism** (Berry et al. 1992). This extreme view is unlikely to be tenable, for the reasons mentioned earlier, hence the debate mainly revolves around the other two possibilities. **Universality** is the view that mental disorders, as outlined in DSM, are found in all cultures, and in essentially the same form, although there may be some variation in expression in different cultures. **Cultural relativism** argues for a much more significant role for culture than does universality, to the extent that syndromes found in some cultures do not appear elsewhere – these are known as **culture-bound syndromes**. There are several different areas of research that can be brought to bear on this issue. Helman (1984) notes that culture may affect mental disorder in four ways:

- it defines what is normal and abnormal in a particular society;
- it may influence the prevalence and expression of particular disorders;
- it may be a cause of the development of particular disorders;
- it may determine the way the disorder is explained and treated in a given culture.

These form the basis for the following discussion.

How culture defines what is normal and abnormal

In this section we are considering the ways in which culture affects our decisions about what is normal and abnormal. At one point in history, for example, certain groups of people in certain societies considered it desirable to flagellate (whip) themselves regularly. Nowadays that would be regarded as undesirable behaviour.

So are there differences between cultures in ideas about mental health? According to Fernando (1995), in many Eastern cultures mental health is associated with integration and harmony with the family, environment, society and religious values. In the West, the aim is self-sufficiency, autonomy, efficiency and the enhancement of self-esteem. When it comes to mental disorder, ideas also differ about what is unusual or unacceptable.

Response to unusual behaviours

In many societies, being possessed by spirits, hallucinating, and speaking in unknown tongues (glossolalia), are acceptable, provided that those behaviours occur in ways that are prescribed by cultural norms. It is when they do not that they may be regarded as problematic. The research described next attempts to demonstrate when this is likely to occur.

Several studies have explored the response of people from other cultures to psychiatric terms such as 'insane', or to descriptions of people who suffer from symptoms such as hallucinations. Africa would appear to have been the location for most research. In Zimbabwe, Gelfand (1964) reported that hallucinations were considered to be 'real' events sent by spirits. Those who experienced them were not rejected by society, showed reduced levels of distress, and good recovery rates. Collomb (1966) in Senegal found 90% recovery rates, for example. Other less developed countries such as Columbia have shown similarly low levels of stigmatisation and good outcomes (WHO 1977). In Nigeria, the Yoruba were presented with vignettes describing case studies of mentally ill persons, one of whom was a paranoid schizophrenic. Almost all Americans would identify such a person as being mentally ill, but only 40% of the Yoruba group did so; 30% said they would be willing to marry such a person (Erinosho & Ayonrinde 1981). Educated Nigerians, however, presented a different picture (Binitie 1970), in that 31% said such a person should be expelled, and 16% said they should be shot. Thus education (and Westernisation) had led to a decrease in tolerance.

Research in Laos (Westermayer & Wintrob 1978) showed that the term 'insane' ('baa') was applied only after several years to disruptive, violent individuals who displayed bizarre behaviours. Hallucinations were not considered a problem. Even those who were considered insane would still be given food, clothing, shelter and care. Edgerton (1971) in East Africa also found that hallucinations were not considered a problem. The term 'psychosis' ('kichaa') was applied to those who commit murder, arson, theft or show themselves naked. Depending on the area, they may be treated with rituals and tranquillising herbs, starved, expelled or battered to death. In Malaya, only violent people will be termed 'mad' ('gila')and banished from the village (Colson 1971).

Differences in interpretation of symptoms

There are also societies in which particular symptoms may be seen in different ways. For example, in Hindu and Buddhist societies depression is not seen as an illness, but as a spiritual insight about the world. Thus it is an accomplishment (Castillo 1991). In Micronesia, depressive feelings are always traced back to some personal loss to do with relationships, and they are seen as normal even if the depression goes on for a long time (Lutz 1985). In Britain, Furnham and Malik (1994) found that middle-aged Asian immigrants did not see depressive symptoms as an illness, whereas a British sample and a sample of younger immigrants from Asia did. In societies that place a high value on ritual purity, e.g. Israel and India, fear of contamination and hand washing may be more acceptable than in the West. In the Swat Pukhtun of Pakistan, which is a violent and competitive culture, paranoia would not be an appropriate diagnosis, since people *do* plot against one another (Castillo 1997). Nor would antisocial personality disorder be considered unusual, since extreme egocentrism is the norm. The 'macho' behaviour associated with histrionic personality disorder in DSM (APA 1994, p. 656) is considered to be appropriate in Latin cultures.

Conclusion

Such research clearly shows that there is only very limited consensus about what is abnormal behaviour. Extreme behaviours, which would in many cases be dealt with by the legal system in Western society, are generally agreed to be unacceptable in most other cultures, but many of the behaviours that we would regard as indicative of severe mental disorder are accepted. Indeed, in some societies they are even accorded high status. Rogler and Hollingshead (1965) report that Puerto Rican schizophrenics may rise in status if they visit a spiritualist, as they are seen to have psychic faculties themselves. They may then become more acceptable as husbands. The differences in prognosis in other cultures also indicate that for such persons in Western society, the disorder itself is only part of their problems.

Progress exercise

Look back at the case studies in Chapter 2. If these individuals lived in other cultures, do you think that their behaviours would be accepted? Would they be able to function adequately if others did not regard them as abnormal?

Differences in prevalence and expression of mental disorders

Cultures and subcultures can be compared in terms of differences in prevalence (rate of occurrence) of mental disorders in the population and in the ways that mental disorders are expressed.

Differences in prevalence in different cultures

Reading about the history of mental disorder reveals that disorders come and go at different historical periods. In the Middle Ages, there were mass outbreaks of lycanthropy – feeling that one is turning into a wolf and growing fur – but this disorder is virtually unheard of nowadays. In late 18th- and early 19th-century Europe somnambulism (sleepwalking) was quite common. Could there be a similar variation between different cultures at the same point in time? Remember that if there is significant variability in frequency of occurrence, this will go against the notion of cultural universality of mental disorder.

The anthropologist Kleinman (1991) noted that many adult disorders such as depression and manic depression, schizophrenia, dementia and anxiety disorders do seem to occur universally. Some studies have been carried out to ascertain whether the prevalence of specific disorders is different in different countries. One problem that faces researchers in this area is whether to accept the diagnoses of practitioners from other cultures (who may use different diagnostic systems, as they do in China, for example), or whether to insist that all diagnoses are carried out by Western-trained clinicians according to our standards. It is very unlikely that the same results will be obtained in the two cases.

Schizophrenia

A study for the World Health Organisation by Sartorius et al. (1986) found that there was in general a 1% risk of developing schizophrenia between the ages of 15–54. However, this varied in different cultures, from as low as 0.53% in Honolulu to as much as 1.74% in rural India. This research has been criticised (Berry et al. 1992) on the grounds that the coverage of cultures was limited, and it may therefore have underestimated the full range of possible variation. There is also the problem of applying Western criteria that do not carry the same negative connotations elsewhere – hallucinations and delusions often represent a belief in the supernatural, for example, which is considered perfectly acceptable in other cultures. Another study (Jablensky et al. 1992) found similar rates of occurrence in 10 countries, including India, Britain, Denmark, Russia, Nigeria, Japan, America, and the Czech republic.

Dissociation

This is regarded as being virtually ubiquitous (Bourguignon 1973), although in most cultures it is seen as being an important part of cultural rituals, rather than a problematic disorder.

Alcoholism

Helzer et al. (1990) compared the rates of alcoholism in five cities in different countries, and found a range in lifetime prevalence for males of between 23% for Koreans to 7% for Taiwanese. This compared with a rate of 19% in Edmonton, Alberta. Given the different cultural usage of alcohol, it is not surprising that there are different risk factors (Catalano et al. 1993). Although some countries have a higher rate of consumption than others (e.g. France), alcohol is typically taken in small amounts with meals over the course of the day. In other countries (e.g. America) it is used at the end of the day for the purposes of intoxication. In others (e.g. Muslim countries) it is expressly forbidden on religious grounds. In Indian, American Indian and Saudi cultures, abstinence is defined as ideal behaviour, and drinking is not a normal part of social life. In Ireland, Japan and Puerto Rico, heavy alcohol use is expected in males, and they would be considered socially impaired if they did not participate.

Anorexia nervosa and bulimia nervosa

These are far more common in modern, industrialised societies such as America, Canada, Europe, Australia, Japan and New Zealand (Ritenbaugh et al. 1992). This difference has been attributed to the culturally promoted images of ideal female beauty in Western countries. A study by Nasser (1986) showed that Egyptian students studying in London were more likely to develop an eating disorder than a group of controls studying in Cairo, which lends some support to this explanation.

Major depressive disorder

Depression does not seem to be much in evidence in Asian cultures. This may well be, according to Rack (1982), because Asians only consult for the physical symptoms associated with depression. The emotional experience, as noted in a previous section, is not seen to be a problem. The prevalence of depression is lower in Taiwan and Hong Kong than in the West (Compton et al. 1991), which has been attributed to the extra social support available in those countries (Tseng et al. 1995).

The Cross-national Collaborative Group (1992) reported that depression is increasing in prevalence generally, and occurring at younger and younger ages, although there is cultural variability. The cumulative rate of occurrence in America, for example, is much higher than that in the Lebanon and Taiwan. Breakdown of social support systems, lack of opportunity for young people and the negative socio-cultural construction of the elderly, are among the explanations offered for the increase in modernised societies.

Anxiety

This presents more evidence of cultural variability, particularly when generalised anxiety is assessed (Tseng et al. 1990). However, there is more agreement with object phobias. Davey et al. (1998) reported agreement on the stimuli that are phobia-related in Japan, Britain, America, Italy, Scandinavia, India, Korea and Hong Kong.

Obsessive-compulsive disorder

The most common forms of this disorder have been found in England, Egypt, India, Israel, Taiwan and Puerto Rico, indicating cultural similarity (Staley & Wand 1995). However, clinicians need to bear in mind the prevailing cultural norms when making a diagnosis, as in many cultures, such as Egypt, India and Israel, ritual purification and washing are important parts of religious observances, and therefore are not considered abnormal.

Conclusion

Research into cultural differences in prevalence was begun in 1904 by the father of modern psychiatry, Emil Kraepelin, who travelled to Java to see if dementia praecox (now known as schizophrenia) and manic depression were found there. His conclusions, like those of many modern researchers, were that there was some universality, and some aspects of disorders that were culturally distinctive. Given the internal diversity of most countries, it should not be too surprising that this is the case, if culture is accepted to have an influence.

Weisz et al. (1987) attempted to explain cultural differences such as those noted earlier with their **suppression-facilitation model**. Based on learning theory principles, they argue that behaviours that are rewarded within a culture will be observed frequently (facilitated), whereas those that are discouraged will be suppressed. Studies of children in America and Thailand who had been referred for the treatment of behaviour problems found that the behaviour they showed most predominantly was an exaggeration of that preferred by the parents. In America this was assertive behaviour, which manifested itself as problem behaviours such as aggression and distractability. In Thailand this was quiet, controlled behaviour, which manifested as overcontrolled behaviour such as anxiety and fearfulness. Thus the cultural values and expectations of the parents had led to different patterns of problem behaviour in the two countries, or more accurately, to different patterns being perceived as problems in the two countries.

Differences in expression in different cultures

Again, it can be seen that there is historical variability in the expression of disorders. A good example of this is multiple personality disorder, which was initially seen in the form of 'double consciousness'. Based perhaps on the Christian concept of good versus evil, early cases in the mid-19th century manifested as two alters. In the modern world, where life is generally more fragmented, cases have been observed with hundreds of alters (Kenny 1986). Could such variability be observed across cultures at the same time?

Schizophrenia has again received the most attention. In developed countries, the disorder seems to occur in a more severe form; 40% of cases are severe compared with 24% in developing countries (Sartorius et al. 1986). This, however, could be due to differences in diagnosis, as some of those seen in the developing countries recovered so quickly that it was unlikely that they were suffering from true schizophrenia in the first place. In 1979, the WHO compared the symptoms of schizo-phrenia in nine different countries. Some symptoms were common: lack of insight was found in 97% of cases seen; hallucinations were found in 70%. However, when the subtypes – paranoid, hebephrenic and catatonic – were explored, differences emerged. Catatonic and hebephrenic types were found to be more common in developing countries such as India, and paranoid types in more urban, Western, developed countries such as Japan (Kleinman & Cohen 1997; Lin 1996).

Other cultures may also show completely different symptoms from those found in Western cases. The Inuit, for example, have a syndrome that appears similar to schizophrenia (e.g. it includes talking to non-existent people) but also includes other symptoms such as killing dogs. The content of schizophrenic delusions will also vary, by definition (Kim et al. 1993). DSM IV (APA 1994) defines bizarre delusions as those that 'are not understandable and do not derive from ordinary life experiences' (p. 275). The supernatural powers accepted by many other cultures may seem bizarre to Western eyes.

Experiences may also be described in different ways. Littlewood and Lipsedge (1989) noted that 40% of psychotic Afro-Caribbean patients describe their experiences in religious terms, compared with only 20% of white British patients. Scheper-Hughes (1979) found that in rural Kerry, Ireland, religious descriptions were more common than in white American schizophrenics. Western psychotics were more likely than psychotics from other cultures to describe their experiences in terms of extra-terrestrials.

Anorexia, when it is found in non-Western countries, does not tend to include the symptoms of distorted body image or fear of being too fat (Lee & Hsu 1995). Since these constitute part of the criteria for diagnosis of the disorder in DSM, it is arguable whether these forms can be regarded as true anorexia (Weiss 1995). Lee et al. (1993) found that the main fear was of stomach bloating rather than fatness in Chinese anorexics. In India, Khandelwal et al. (1995) did not find disturbances of body image or excessive exercising, nor was there fear of fatness. Food intake was restricted on the basis of powerful religious or nutritional beliefs.

Depression

This also shows variability. In 1983, the WHO found that depressive patients from Canada, Iran, India, Japan and Switzerland showed different symptoms: 68% of the Swiss sample showed guilt feelings, and only 22% of the Iranians did, for example; 57% of the Iranians showed somatisation (physical symptoms such as headaches, weight loss, pains etc), whereas only 27% of the Canadians did. In general, somatisation is more common in the Far East and in patients of lower socio-economic status (Kleinman 1980). The Taiwanese, for example, are very reluctant to express personal feelings and thoughts. Lau et al. (1983) in Hong Kong reported that the chief complaints leading depressive patients to seek help were gastric discomfort (18.7%), dizziness (12.2%), headaches (9.8%) and insomnia (8.4%). Of their sample, 96% initially complained of somatic symptoms, and hardly any mentioned emotional problems. In Britain, depressed Asian immigrants are most likely to complain of generalised weakness, bowel problems, fear of heart attack and concern about their genitals (Hussain & Gomersall 1978). In Turkey, too, it has been found that somatic complaints such as insomnia and hypochondria are more common (Ulusahin et al. 1994). In Britain, guilt and pessimism are common. Thoughts about suicide and suicide rates are also variable. Barraclough (1988) showed Scandinavia, Eastern Europe and some Asian countries to be highest in this respect, and the Arab countries to be the lowest.

Conclusion

When Western categories of mental disorder are recognised in other cultures, they frequently show quite marked differences in symptomatology. This makes the universal application of DSM diagnostic categories difficult.

Subcultural differences

In this section we will look at differences in four subcultural categories: ethnic groups; gender; class; and age. An important general point in this context is that there may be many possible explanations for any differences observed. At the very least, they may be explained by differences in help-seeking behaviour, or by bias in the assessment process and/or classification system, as well as by genuine differences in prevalence. Even genuine differences in prevalence may be the result of poor social conditions or the stress associated with prejudice, rather than being biologically based. It is also very difficult for research to separate out the effects of the ethnicity, class, age and gender of participants.

Ethnic groups

DIFFERENCES IN HELP-SEEKING

Before we look at the statistics, it can be stated at the outset that there are differences here in the extent to which ethnic groups use health services. Some encourage individuals to seek professional help, others insist upon the denial of problems; some tolerate problem behaviours, others develop physical symptoms and seek medical help for those rather than for their emotional problems. In America, it has been found that African ethnic groups use services more and Hispanic and Asian groups use services less, compared with Caucasians. Orientals are more likely to seek medical help than psychological help (Sue et al. 1991).

Kendall and Hammen (1995) attribute these differences to variation in cultural attitudes about such problems and where to seek help. Another possible explanation has been proposed by Kirmayer et al. (1996) in Montreal, who found that when levels of psychological distress were controlled, immigrants were ¼ to ⅓ less likely to seek mental health care. When questioned about this, the most important factor was found to be 'ethnic mismatch'. By this the immigrants meant their expectations that they would be unable to see profes-sionals from their own ethnic group, that they would not be understood by those they did see, and that they would encounter prejudice. In Britain, Frederick (1991) reported that Black persons participating in the study were less likely to have sought help of their own accord. Afro-Caribbean women have also been found to be more critical of

GPs, and Afro-Caribbeans are also less likely than other groups to be referred for help by GPs (Pilgrim & Rogers 1999).

RATES WITHIN IMMIGRANT GROUPS

Looking at general levels of mental health, Guarnaccia et al. (1990) compared Puerto Ricans living in Puerto Rico with those living in cities in America. The rates of disorder and reported symptoms appear to be higher in the immigrant groups, and higher in Puerto Ricans than in other disadvantaged groups. The researchers argued that this is due to the culturally accepted way of responding to stress in Puerto Rico. Called 'ataque de nervios', this involves fainting, seizures and heart palpitations (see later). Clinicians may well interpret such symptoms as being indicative of mental health problems if they use the current classification system without making any allowance for the effects of culture.

In Britain, Cochrane (1977) found that the psychiatric admission rates for Polish, Irish and Scottish immigrants to England and Wales were higher than for those born in those countries. Early research into other ethnic groups, such as Asians and Afro-Caribbeans, produced conflicting findings, but more recent, better-controlled studies are more consistent, although the picture is still variable for Asian groups. For example, Carpenter and Brockington (1980) found higher admission rates for Asian groups, while Hitch (1981) found that Pakistani-born groups had higher rates and Indian-born groups had lower rates. This may be due to comparing them with different control groups, however; the first study used White Britons, and the second Asians born in Britain.

STRESS OR SELECTION?

Immigrants may also represent a special case, since immigration itself may be a stressful process (stress hypothesis) and those who choose to do it may have more problems than most (selection hypothesis).

There is some support for both of these explanations. As regards the latter, Schaechter (1965) in Australia found that 45.5% of a sample of immigrants admitted to psychiatric hospitals had a record of mental illness prior to migrating. This figure was increased to 68.2% when possible cases were included as well. As regards the former, the difficulties faced by immigrants can perhaps be most clearly seen in the Irish statistics. Irish immigrants to mainland Britain have been shown by Cochrane and Bal (1989) to have the highest incidence of diagnosis for most categories of disorder – psychoses, neuroses, depression, personality disorder and alcohol abuse. Psychiatric admissions, for example, are 1080 per 100,000 compared to 504 per 100,000 for English people. Pilgrim and Rogers (1999) attribute this to two groups of factors: first, material factors such as poverty, forced migration and unstable social and political conditions; and second, cultural factors such as oppression by the church and a history of English colonialism, both of which have led to crises of identity for the Irish people. Littlewood and Lipsedge (1989) argue that different immigrant groups have different risk factors due to their specific circumstances. Some appear to be more at risk than others, such as Afro-Caribbeans. Refugees, who are often forced to leave their country, suffer trauma before leaving and cannot return, may be particularly at risk.

RATES IN DIFFERENT ETHNIC GROUPS

Another approach is to look at the rates of disorder in ethnic groups compared with those of the population as a whole. Looking at Afro-Caribbeans, they appear to be consistently overrepresented in psychiatric hospital admissions (McGovern & Cope 1987) given their numbers in the population in general. According to Banyard (1996) Black people only account for 5% of the population, but they constitute 25% of those in psychiatric hospitals. Although hospital admissions are not generally good indicators of the rates of occurrence of disorder, these findings are borne out by a study by Harrison et al. (1988), which included all patients in contact with psychiatric services.

Explanations offered for these findings have tended to attribute the difficulties faced by Afro-Caribbeans to poverty and racism (e.g. Littlewood & Lipsedge 1989). The relatively lower rates of admission in Asian communities (compared to those of Afro-Caribbeans) may be attributable to greater affluence, a more fatalistic attitude to life, or the greater stigma associated with help-seeking in Asian communities. However, such explanations cannot account for the observed differences in Irish and other groups, nor for the differences in the type of disorder noted, which is the topic we move on to next.

DIFFERENCES IN TYPE OF DISORDER

Many studies have now confirmed that the rate of occurrence of schizophrenia in Afro-Caribbeans in Britain is considerably higher than it is in the general population, that such differences are also found in second-generation immigrants and that they do not occur in Afro-Caribbeans who have emigrated to other countries. For example, Cochrane and Sashidharan (1995) report a seven-fold increase in incidence. Harrison et al. (1988) estimated it to be 12–13 times that of the general population. In America the rates of admission for schizophrenia have been reported to be approximately double for Black males compared with the general population. This may also apply to Hispanic Americans (Mukherjee et al. 1983), Inuit (Sampath 1974) and American Indians (Roy et al. 1970).

Nor are these the only differences observed. Substance abuse, for example, is more common in African Americans than Whites (Flaskerud 2000), and alcoholism is more common in American Indians (Kendall & Hammen 1995). Attempted suicide is a particular problem in British Asian women (Gross & McIlveen 1998). These latter conditions, however, are more objectively verifiable than schizophrenia, and more readily attributable to social conditions and lifestyles.

WHY ARE THERE DIFFERENT RATES FOR SCHIZOPHRENIA?

So how can the differential rates of schizophrenia be explained? Pilgrim and Rogers (1999) suggest two processes: misdiagnosis and ethnocentric psychiatric constructs.

Misdiagnosis is the misapplication of psychiatric labels, which could result from the ethnocentric views of the (usually White) psychiatrists dealing with such cases. Blake (1973) found that a case study that included a description of the patient as African American was more likely to be given a label of schizophrenia by clinicians than the same case study described as a white person. Thus Black and White people are seen differently even when they show the same behaviour. Loring and Powell (1988) found the same applied even when the clinicians were themselves Black. Fernando (1991) points out that White (or even Black) middle-class psychiatrists are unlikely to have any experience of the culture or general social conditions in which their clients are immersed. For example, Bell (2000), reviewing studies of the exposure of Black children in American inner cities to violence, quoted research by Fitzpatrick and Boldizar (1993) showing that 70% of their sample had witnessed a shooting and 44% had seen a murder.

Ethnocentric psychiatric constructs derive from taking a Western viewpoint when devising the classification systems themselves. These systems can be viewed as social constructs, or as Fernando (1988) puts it '**psychiatric imperialism**'. Thus the norms for behaviour are based on Western expectations, and so deviations from those, such as hearing voices or going into trances, must be abnormal irrespective of the culture of the person concerned.

CONCLUSION.

Clearly, then, even within this small area of research, there are some very complex forces at work, and the observed differences cannot readily be attributed to one single factor. Cultural norms regarding acceptance of behaviours and help-seeking, stress and clinical bias may all be responsible. What can be concluded, however, is that in one way or another, many of the factors involved do relate to culture.

Gender

DIFFERENCES.

Statistics relating to psychiatric hospital admissions for men and women in both England and America show similar patterns. The English statistics are given in Table 4.1. Overall, women are more at risk than men of suffering from a mental disorder. There are, however, significant differences between disorders. Women are particularly at risk of suffering from affective psychoses (e.g. depression), neurotic disorders (especially phobias and panic disorders), borderline personality disorder and dementia, and 90–95% of anorexics and bulimics are female. Men are more at risk from alcohol abuse, antisocial personality disorder, pyromania, gambling problems, obsessive-compulsive disorder and (marginally) schizophrenia. These differences appear to be reducing compared with their levels in 1976. They are also far from being universal; in China, for example, women show higher rates of schizophrenia than men, and lower rates of depression and neurosis than Western women (Pearson 1995). Cross culturally, men show a slightly greater incidence of depression than women (Carstairs & Kapur 1976). However, the differences are still significant enough to warrant investigation.

Table 4.1 Rates of admission to hospitals in England in 1986 per 100,000 population by sex and diagnostic group. From *A Sociology of Mental Health and Illness, 2nd edition* by D. Pilgrim and A. Rogers, Open University Press, 1999 with the permission of Open University Press

Diagnosis	Males	Females	Excess of female over male rate (%)
All diagnoses	364	468	+29
Schizophrenia	66	58	−12
Affective psychoses	35	68	+98
Other psychoses	32	44	+37
Senile and presenile dementia	33	55	+67
Alcohol psychoses and alcoholism	45	20	−55
Drug dependence	9	8	−11
Neurotic disorders	22	42	+91
Personality and behaviour disorders	28	32	+14
Other conditions[1]	89	142	+60
Rates for all diagnoses (1986)	364	468	+29
Rates for all diagnoses (1976)	320	447	+40

[1] This category includes depression not classified elsewhere

EXPLANATIONS.

Several explanations can be considered. First, there is the possibility that the differences observed are biologically based. It has been argued, for example, that women are less prone to schizophrenia than men because they are protected by the hormone oestrogen. The equal rates for schizophrenia in persons who are beyond menopausal age would suggest that this could be the case, but there is little other evidence to support this explanation (Prentice 1996). Hormonal fluctuations in women during the menstrual cycle, in pregnancy and as a result of the use of contraceptives have also been blamed for depression, but again the evidence is far from conclusive (Weissman & Klerman 1981). For example, Cooper et al. (1988) found a slight increase in depression in women who had just given birth, but it was still lower than that in non-pregnant women. Given the range of differences observed, several biological mechanisms would need to be postulated, and it seems unlikely that this would be the case.

A second possibility is that women express distress in different ways from men. The Western gender roles allow women to be emotional, whereas men are expected to be dominant, independent, rational and controlled. Women are expected to be concerned about weight and appearance, whereas men are expected to pursue their goals aggressively. These differences would seem to fit in with the observed patterns as regards different disorders.

Another view would be that they reflect differences in help-seeking behaviour. Women generally seek help, both medical and psychological, more often than men do for the same disorders (Shapiro et al. 1984). Men have often been referred to as suffering from the 'John Wayne syndrome', meaning that the gender stereotype to which they are expected to conform precludes them from seeking help, especially for psychiatric problems. Since the research generally relies on hospital admissions or community surveys of use of mental health services at best, this is a significant problem and cannot be dismissed. However, it cannot account for the different types of disorder noted. Recent studies also indicate that women do not always recognise mental health problems such as post-natal depression as significant enough to lead to help-seeking (Whitton et al. 1996).

A fourth explanation relates to social causation of the differences. Here a variety of mechanisms have been postulated. Cochrane (1995) notes that the rate of child abuse for girls is much higher than that for boys, and that up to 70% of depressed patients admitted to hospitals have suffered abuse as children. That, combined with the general incidence of abuse (up to 46% of children may be affected, according to some estimates) Cochrane considers sufficient to account for the gender differences in levels of depression. Brown et al. (1995) found that ⅓ of the sample of depressed women they studied had suffered neglect or physical or sexual abuse during childhood. Brown (1996) suggests that such experiences also increase the chance of suffering from anxiety in adulthood, and could account for the finding that depression and anxiety are often found together. Williams et al. (1993) found that at least 50% of women using the mental health services they reviewed had been sexually and/or physically abused as children and/or as adults.

Other life experiences that relate to gender roles have been implicated. Women's roles are frequently linked with powerlessness, submissiveness and lack of opportunity to achieve except vicariously through their husbands. These are conditions associated with the concept of learned helplessness (Seligman 1973), which produces behaviour akin to depression in animals. The circumstances in which this may be most marked are those noted by Brown and Harris (1978) in their findings on risk factors for depression in women – lack of employment outside the home, presence of three or more children under the age of 15 years, absence of a confiding relationship with a partner and loss of mother before the age of 11 years (which is also one factor associated with an increased likelihood of child abuse). Low self-esteem, chronic social difficulties such as shortage of money, and feeling humiliated and trapped by the situation (Unger 1984) also contribute to the problem. Cochrane (1995) adds that whereas men cope with such problems by active achievement (e.g. at work), by obtaining social support (usually from women) or by substance abuse, depression may be the more likely form of coping in women. It could be, for example, that it is more acceptable in view of their gender roles.

It should not be forgotten in this connection that the male figures also require an explanation. Schizophrenia is slightly more likely in men than in women overall, but between the ages of 15 and 24 it is twice as likely (Warner 1985). It has been suggested (Pilgrim & Rogers 1999) that this may be because this is the time when work and career-related stress are at their peak. Men are particularly vulnerable to suffering psychiatric problems as a consequence of unemployment (Johnstone 1989).

The fifth explanation of the gender differences would be that clinicians are biased in the way that they diagnose mental disorders. Broverman et al. (1981) found that if clinicians were asked to identify the characteristics of the healthy man, the healthy woman and the healthy adult, they placed women in a separate group, describing them as ideally dependent, submissive and emotional. Men and adults were independent, assertive and decisive. Looking specifically at diagnoses, Ford and Widiger (1989) gave clinicians case studies describing histrionic personality disorder and antisocial personality disorder. Each case study was labelled as either male or female when presented to different clinicians, and they were asked to diagnose the conditions. When labelled as male, antisocial personality disorder was correctly identified 40% of the time, compared with under 20% of the time when labelled as female. Histrionic personality disorder was correctly diagnosed 80% of the time when labelled as female, and around 30% of the time when labelled as male. Thus the behaviours were interpreted in accordance with the expectations for that gender – women should be emotional (histrionic) and men should be aggressive (antisocial).

Finally, it is also possible that the classification system itself is biased. For some syndromes, the diagnostic descriptions appear to link closely with typical behaviours of one gender or the other. It should not therefore be too surprising that those syndromes are more commonly diagnosed in those genders. Chesler (1972) goes further than this, and argues that the female role demands behaviours that are clinically neurotic; rejection of the role, on the other hand, is seen as deviance. As Busfield (1996, p. 101) puts it, 'Women are likely to be viewed as disturbed if they "act out" either masculine or feminine roles; men only if they act out feminine roles.' There is a double standard for mental health, with the result that women will inevitably show a higher level of disorder – exactly what the statistics show.

Social class

DIFFERENCES.

There is variation in the incidence of most disorders according to social class. The Midtown Manhattan Study by Srole et al. (1962) was one of the first to show that the lowest levels of psychiatric disorder could be found in the upper classes, and the highest in the lower classes. In Britain, Cochrane and Stopes-Roe (1981) obtained the same findings. Bruce et al. (1991) found that over a 6-month period a sample of people living below the poverty line were more than twice as likely as others to have developed a substance abuse disorder, or an affective disorder, and 80 times as likely to have developed schizophrenia. Many other studies have confirmed that the major disorders such as schizophrenia are more likely to occur in the lower social classes. For example, Faris and Dunham (1939) found schizophrenia to be seven times more likely in poor inner-city dwellers than in those from middle-class suburbia. The same results have been found in Denmark, Norway and England.

Suicide (Taylor et al. 1996), and substance abuse (Meltzer et al. 1995) are more common in the unskilled and unemployed. Depression (Brown 1996) and Alzheimer's disease (Ott et al. 1995) are also more common in the lower classes. Manic depression may be more common in the middle classes. Also more common in the middle classes are the neurotic disorders, and anorexia nervosa.

EXPLANATIONS

Again, several explanations have been considered. First, there is the **social drift hypothesis**, which suggests that persons suffering from severe mental disorders will move down the social scale because of the debilitating effects the disorder has on their ability to function. Thus being low-class is a consequence of the disorder, not a cause. Schizophrenia, for example, may begin later in life than some other disorders, and the individual may have had a successful career prior to its onset. The evidence here is inconclusive, however. Hollingshead and Redlich (1958) did not find any evidence for drift. Goldberg and Morrison (1963) found that the fathers of schizophrenics were of a higher social class, indicating downward mobility; Turner and Wagonfeld (1967), on the other hand, found that even the fathers were low, which would limit the scope for downward mobility.

Second, there is the **sociogenic hypothesis**, which argues that social conditions are responsible for the differences observed. According to this, poverty, unemployment, poorer physical health and environmental conditions all add up to increased levels of stress in the lower classes, who may in addition have fewer coping resources at their disposal and may feel less in control of their lives. The middle classes can afford pleasurable experiences such as holidays to alleviate their stress, for example, and may more readily be able to obtain social support or seek professional help. Halpern (1995) notes that there is an increase in mental disorder in those living in high-rise blocks; this may be due to social class, or simply to the fact that in such blocks there is less social contact. Wilkinson (1996) points to the perception of inequalities as a source of considerable stress, especially when it is combined with lack of control or ability to take effective action to change one's circumstances. Brown and Harris (1978) found that a high level of stress tended to be associated with a high level of mental disorder in general. Fryer (1995) found that unemployment increases the chance of mental disorder not only in the individual concerned, but also in other family members.

In order to test the two latter explanations, Dohrenwend et al. (1992) compared established groups of European immigrants to Israel with recent groups of African and Middle Eastern immigrants who would have suffered more prejudice. For schizophrenia, they found that the social drift hypothesis was supported, in that the former group showed higher rates, especially those in the lower social classes. Social causation was linked with higher rates of depression in women, and substance abuse and antisocial personality disorder in men in the latter, disadvantaged groups. Thus it may be that different explanations apply to different disorders.

The final explanation relates to clinical bias. It is also possible that clinicians give less favourable diagnoses to those people from the lower social classes. Umbenhauer and DeWitte (1978) confirmed this, and also showed that upper-class patients were more likely to be offered psychotherapy rather than pharmacotherapy. In a review of the research, Johnstone (1989) found that people from the lower social classes were regarded as being less able to benefit from verbal therapies, because they were less articulate, and were often given a poorer prognosis.

Age

DIFFERENCES

Certain disorders are so strongly associated with particular age groups that they are described as such in the classification system; disorders of childhood (such as autism) and old age (such as dementia) constitute distinct categories. However, the expectations that people have of children will differ according to culture, as shown by Whiting and Edwards (1988) in a study of six different cultures. For many other disorders, there is the implication that the behaviour displayed is inappropriate for a person of a particular age. Children may talk to imaginary friends, for example, but adults may not. Most disorders, such as depression and anxiety, could occur at any stage of the life cycle. Depression is in fact uncommon in children below the age of about 9 years. Carlson and Cantwell (1980) argue that this is because they cannot express their feelings in ways that clinicians would understand, and that would relate to the diagnostic criteria. Major depression has been found to increase in incidence between 15 and 19 (in females particularly), and in those over 90 (Burke et al. 1990). The median age of onset for bipolar disorder, panic disorder, obsessive-compulsive disorder, phobias, substance abuse, schizophrenia and antisocial personality disorder has also been found to be around late adolescence/early adulthood. In Britain the prevalence of depression has been found to be around 11–15% in the over 65s (Copeland et al. 1987). In old people's homes this may rise to 38% (Mann et al. 1984).

EXPLANATIONS

As with the other differences we have discussed, there are a variety of possible explanations. The first group relate to social and physical conditions. For example, it has been argued that in young adulthood there are more pressures – educational, occupational and social – and young people do not always have the experience to cope with them all. Old people, on the other hand, are often suffering from physical illnesses as well, which will inevitably reduce their satisfaction with life. Dover and McWilliam (1992) found that in their sample of elderly depressed patients only 3% of men and 20% of women were physically well. Many had serious complaints such as cancer or cardiovascular illness. The drugs given for these conditions may in turn lead to depression.

Older people also suffer from other social conditions that may be associated with depression. Those in residential homes may suffer from lack of stimulation, as well as loss of personal autonomy and control over the environment in which they live. Material adversity, and loss of social relationships, may also occur. Blaxter (1990) found, for example, that the psychosocial well-being of older people is associated with social class. Lowenthal et al. (1965) found that having a stable confiding relationship protected elderly people against depression. As many as 30% of those reporting the lack of such a relationship have been found to be depressed.

Another view would be that the diagnostic system is itself biased, as Carlson and Cantwell (1980) argue with respect to young children. Research into the clinical experiences of the elderly is lacking, since they have been excluded from most of the research carried out to date (which could in itself be viewed as a bias).

Conclusion

This section has demonstrated that across cultures there are marked differences in the recorded prevalence of different mental disorders, and in the way that disorders are expressed. These differences can also be seen at the subcultural level in different ethnic, gender, social class and age groups within a culture. Some explanations have been considered for these observed differences, but they are likely to be complex and multi-causal. In the next section we will examine the evidence for culture-bound syndromes.

Culture-bound syndromes

One innovative feature of DSM IV compared with its predecessor DSM IIIR is that it has made explicit attempts to address cultural issues. A National Institute of Mental Health working group was set up to look into the issues of culture and diagnosis when DSM IV was being drawn up. As a result, version IV includes an outline for cultural formulation and a glossary of culture-bound syndromes. The first of these is an attempt to help clinicians to apply the DSM criteria in a multicultural environment. It suggests that the clinician should take into account the individual's cultural background by making notes on the person's cultural identity, cultural explanations of the presenting illness (e.g. spiritual possession), culturally relevant social factors (e.g. stressors, social support), cultural elements of the relationship between the individual and the clinician, and cultural considerations related to diagnosis and care. The DSM glossary attempts to provide an account of syndromes that are not found in all cultures, and it is this we are concerned with here. We will also consider Western (DSM) syndromes that do not occur elsewhere, and criticisms of the cultural formulation of DSM.

Definition

Culture-bound syndromes are defined by DSM (APA 1994, p. 844) as 'recurrent, locality-specific patterns of aberrant behaviour and troubling experience that may or may not be linked to a particular DSM-IV diagnostic category.' This definition has been criticised for its vagueness, which can be seen in the use of terms such as 'aberrant' and 'troubling', and in particular the phrase 'locality-specific'. The last, for example, does not clarify how to deal with syndromes that are not universal but are nevertheless found in a range of different areas. The syndromes identified by DSM include the following:

Amok is a south-east Asian trance or dissociative syndrome that occurs only in males and is characterised by a period of depressive brooding, often precipitated by an insult and accompanied by persecutory ideas. This is followed by a violent, often homicidal outburst that may last for several hours and ends in a state of exhaustion. Amnesia for the episode follows. In Laos, some Polynesian islands and the Philippines it is known as 'cafard'. Locally, it is attributed to interpersonal conflict and loss of honour (Carr 1985).

Ataque de nervios is associated with Latin cultures in America and the Mediterranean. It occurs most frequently in women, but can also be found in men. It involves extreme anxiety, shortness of breath, crying, trembling, numbness in the hands, aggression and possibly fainting, convulsions or suicidal gestures. It may occur as a result of a stressful experience such as a bereavement, and there may be amnesia for the episode later. The attack is often attributed indigenously to an attack by evil spirits, as well as to grief or conflict. An example is given in Box 4.1.

Bilis/colera involve nervous tension, headaches, trembling, screaming, loss of consciousness and stomach disturbances, followed by chronic fatigue. This occurs in Latin cultures and is associated with strong feelings of rage.

BOX 4.1 A case study of ataque de nervios (Spitzer et al. 1994)

The patient was a Dominican female who was being treated in America. She seemed very frightened, alternately screaming, remaining silent or mumbling to herself. She also heard voices telling her to kill herself. At times, she would try to snatch valuables from other patients. It emerged that she had recently been told that her ex-husband had remarried, and she was afraid of being left unsupported. When she found out that he would still pay her child support, her symptoms disappeared.

Boufee delirante is found in West Africa and Haiti. It is characterised by an outburst of agitation and aggression, associated with confusion, hallucinations and paranoia.

Brain fag is found in West African students, who complain of difficulties in concentrating, thinking and remembering, associated with somatic symptoms such as blurring of vision, and feelings of pressure or heat in the head.

Dhat is an Indian syndrome associated with anxiety, depression, fatigue, headaches, loss of appetite and suicidal feelings. It is attributed locally to the loss of semen, which is described in Sanskrit literature as being one of the essential elements that make up the physical body (Singh 1985). Thus excessive masturbation or sexual intercourse could lead to these symptoms. Western-trained psychiatrists often diagnose this as major depression (Singh 1985). A case study is given in Box 4.2.

Falling out occurs in Black persons in southern America and the Caribbean, and involves a sudden collapse. The person affected lies with eyes open but is unable to move. They report that they can hear what is going on around them, but cannot see (Weidman 1979). In Haiti this is known as 'indisposition'.

Ghost sickness is found in American Indians, and is characterised by a preoccupation with death and deceased persons. Symptoms include bad dreams, feelings of danger, fainting, anxiety, hallucinations, loss of appetite and a feeling of suffocation.

> **BOX 4.2 A case study of Dhat syndrome (Castillo 1997)**
>
> The client was a 45-year-old clothing merchant, married with four children. He began to masturbate every day when he was a student, and started to worry that he was losing too much semen. In later life, if he had intercourse with his wife too often he developed the symptoms of depression and the physical symptoms associated with Dhat syndrome. He himself felt that his early overindulgence and constant daydreaming of sexual activity had led to him developing bad habits involving too much sexuality. This made him physically weak, and mentally weak to an even greater extent.

Hwa-byung is a Korean syndrome that shows itself as fatigue, depression, insomnia, panic, anorexia, indigestion and aches and pains (Pang 1990). It is attributed to conflict in relationships, and other sources of unexpressed anger, and hence is often referred to as 'anger syndrome'. It is most common in middle-aged women who have little education and domineering husbands or mothers-in-law. Such women are expected to fulfil their role as wife without complaint, and are not allowed to express anger towards either husband or in-laws.

Koro is seen in south-east Asia and southern China and is a recognised syndrome in the Chinese Classification of Mental Disorders. The sufferer fears that the penis, vulva or breasts are shrinking back into the body, and will cause death (Leng 1985). Men may resort to tying a string around the penis to try and prevent this happening. Koro leads to extreme anxiety, fainting, palpitations, sweating and numbness in limbs. It often occurs as a localised epidemic. Indigenously, it is attributed to excessive or inappropriate sexual intercourse, or exposure of the penis to cold. Although it appears to resemble panic or another anxiety disorder, Tseng et al. (1992) found that the personality profile of koro patients differed from that of a group of patients with anxiety disorders in significant ways.

Latah is found in many places in south-east Asia, including Malaya, the Philippines, Japan and Siberia. It is a trance syndrome shown as a response to fright, and includes automatic obedience, echolalia (repetition of the speech of others), imitation of the movements of others, violent body movements and striking out (Simons 1985).

Locura is a severe chronic psychotic disorder that includes symptoms such as incontinence, agitation, hallucinations and unpredictable violent outbursts. It is a term applied in Latin America, and the condition is attributed to life events and inherited vulnerability.

Mal de Ojo is an illness in Mediterranean, Muslim and Latin cultures that is attributed to the 'evil eye', a glance from an envious person. Found mostly in children and females, it involves diarrhoea, vomiting, crying for no reason, fever and disrupted sleep patterns.

Pibloktoq (Arctic hysteria) occurs in Inuit communities, and is more frequent in women . It starts with a period of withdrawal or irritability that may last for hours or days. There is then a dissociative episode lasting from 5 minutes to 1 hour involving extreme excitement, during which the individual may tear off their clothes, scream incoherently, break furniture, eat faeces or run out onto the ice naked. This may be followed by convulsions and coma for up to 12 hours, after which there is amnesia for the event. Indigenously it is attributed to intense fear or personal abuse, real or imagined. According to Dick (1995) there are only around 25 published accounts of this syndrome, and it may well be that those were the result of sexual exploitation of Inuit women by explorers.

Qi-gong psychotic reaction is also included in the Chinese Classification of Mental Disorders. It is a brief episode of psychotic, dissociative or non-psychotic symptoms that follows excessive participation in the Chinese practice of qi-gong (movement and breathing exercises, relaxation and sensory awareness techniques that aim to tone muscles, boost circulation and brain activity and shape the spirit).

Rootwork/voodoo death/mal puesto are symptoms such as anxiety, chest pains or gastrointestinal disorders that result from fear of witchcraft or voodoo in which a curse has been placed on the sufferer by a sorcerer. It occurs in the southern states of America, and in Latin and Caribbean cultures.

Sangue dormido is found in Portuguese Cape Verde Islanders and involves numbness, paralysis, convulsions, heart attacks, infections and miscarriages.

Shenjing shuairuo (neurasthenia) is another disorder recognised in China, and consists of fatigue, dizziness, headaches, memory and concentration loss, and sleep, gastrointestinal and sexual disturbances. It accounts for over half of all psychiatric outpatients in China.

Shenkui is also Chinese, and refers to a syndrome where there are anxiety or panic symptoms together with somatic symptoms such as dizziness, backache, fatigue, insomnia and sexual dysfunction. It is attributed to excessive semen loss through intercourse, masturbation or the loss in white urine. This is felt by sufferers to be a loss of vital life essence and therefore dangerous.

Shin-byung is Korean, and starts with anxiety and somatic complaints such as gastrointestinal disorders, which then lead to dissociation. It is attributed to possession by ancestral spirits.

Spell is a trance state found in southern America, during which the individual communicates with the spirits of the dead. Brief personality change may also occur.

Susto (or 'magical fright') is a Hispanic and Latin American syndrome that combines anxiety, depression, dissociative and somatic symptoms, including vomiting, anorexia, sweating, phobia and irritability. It is attributed to soul loss after a frightening experience (although it may not occur until some years after the event), which has caused the soul to wander and become detached from the body (Bolton 1981) and death is thought to result if treatment is not given to return the soul.

Taijin kyofusho is Japanese, and is a phobia that the body is offensive to others in terms of appearance, smell or movement (Simons & Hughes 1985). It leads to social withdrawal, and is included in the official Japanese Classification of Disorders. Anthropophobia appears to be the Chinese equivalent; it is a fear of being looked at.

Zar is found in Ethiopia, Sudan, Iran, Egypt and other countries in the North African region. It refers to possession by spirits, which may lead to apathy and withdrawal, including refusal to eat or to work, shouting, weeping and singing, or dissociative experiences. However, zar is not seen as a problem locally.

The above disorders are all listed in the appendix on culture-bound syndromes in DSM IV, but there are others. For example, grisi siknis is found in the Indian culture of Nicaragua, and is a trance syndrome that involves assaulting others and self-mutilating with machetes. This is attributed to spirit possession (Dennis 1985). Nangiarpok is an Inuit syndrome that involves intense fear of capsizing and drowning in a kayak, which can lead to social withdrawal and suicide.

Evaluation

The debate here is between whether all cultures basically display the same disorders (universalism) or whether there are real differences in the disorders found in different cultures (relativism).

Universalism

Some writers dispute the existence of the above syndromes as distinct disorders. They take the view that mental disorders are universal and do not show cultural differences. For example, Kiev (1972) considers that they can be adequately categorised within the other DSM axes. Koro and susto can be seen as types of anxiety disorder, voodoo death as a phobia and amok as a dissociative state. Ataque de nervios may be considered to be a brief psychotic episode. If this is accepted, then the Western categories are universal. Another view (Foster & Anderson 1978) is that they should be seen as distinct symptom patterns rather than as diagnostic categories; in this view the diagnostic categories themselves are universal.

The case for cultural differences is weakened because the extent to which many culture-bound syndromes are recognised within the cultural group concerned still needs to be established in many cases. For example, Windigo psychosis (a depressive disorder in which sufferers believe that they have mutated into cannibalistic monsters) had been identified in North American Indians; Marano (1982) subsequently argued that it had never existed.

Allied to this is the issue of establishing reliably what the syndrome entails and which symptoms are typical. Guarnaccia et al. (1996), for example, were able to show that although seizures and suicidal gestures have been associated with ataque de nervios, they only occur in about ⅓ of cases. There may also be identifiable subtypes, and social conditions that are associated with onset may be determined. Ataque de nervios, for example, is associated with unemployed, divorced women over 45 with little educational background, who have recently lost a family member (Guarnaccia, 1993). Another view on this would be that many culture-bound syndromes are in fact very similar. McCajor

141

Hall (1998) has classified them into 10 groups according to symptoms – e.g. possession, mass assault and exhaustion syndromes.

It has also been found that some of the culture-bound syndromes may in fact occur elsewhere; that is to say, they are not culture-bound at all. Tobin (1996), for example, has reported on a case of koro in an Irish male. (See Chapter 6 for details of this study.)

Relativism

Other critics, arguing the case for cultural relativism, consider that incorporation of these syndromes into DSM requires too much distortion of the existing categories. They have also pointed out that DSM IV has not met its goals of being a multicultural document. There are several reasons why this is the case:

- Many of the proposals of the working group were not incorporated in the new DSM IV document (Mezzich et al. 1999), particularly those emphasising the importance of social context when determining diagnosis and treatment.
- Some syndromes do seem to be widely accepted in other cultures. For example, Canino et al. (1987) established in a large-scale study in Puerto Rico that 16% of the population had suffered an ataque de nervios.
- There is an assumption that the Western syndromes represent the standard (Fernando 1991), and those of other cultures are presented as 'exotic' or anomalous; as such, they are only presented as a brief glossary of 25 syndromes drawn from a much larger list (Simons & Hughes 1985). McCajor Hall (1998) lists 36, although it may be the case that, as described earlier, many of these can be grouped together.
- The possibility that any of the Western syndromes may also be 'culture-bound' has been largely overlooked. For example, anorexia nervosa (Prince 1983) and premenstrual syndrome (Johnstone 1987) are relatively infrequent elsewhere in the world.
- There is still little acceptance of cultural variation within societies rather than between them (Acharyya 1996). Class, for example, and age, still receive little attention. This suggests an even greater role for relativism, but raises the issue of how far it is possible or necessary to take such differentiation.

A synthesis

Fernando (1991) argues that rather than seeing culture-bound syndromes as those where culture has distorted the way the disorder manifests itself, the term should be used as 'a shorthand for identifying a condition where a cultural understanding . . . is a sine qua non for bringing any practical help to the individual that is identified as "suffering" from the syndrome.'

It may also be possible to see mental disorders, including both Western and culture-bound syndromes, as falling along a continuum. This could range from those that are locally recognised and do not appear to correspond to syndromes that are more generally observed (e.g. amok), through to those that may so correspond (e.g. ataque de nervios). Outside this group would be other disorders that may subsequently prove not to exist at all, e.g. windigo.

Conclusion

Cultural variability can be observed in the types of mental disorder that occur. However, it is disputed whether these syndromes represent distinct disorders, which DSM has failed to acknowledge adequately, or whether they should be subsumed within the existing system.

For each of the countries/regions/ethnic groups given below, give the names of the culture-bound syndromes that may be associated with them:

Japan; China; Korea; south-east Asia; Africa; India; Caribbean; Latin countries; American Indian; Inuit.

Progress exercise

Differential treatment according to culture

Although detailed coverage of treatment issues is beyond the scope of this book (see *Therapeutic Approaches in Psychology* by Susan Cave), it is useful to conclude this chapter with a brief consideration of the implications for treatment of the cultural variations we have been discussing. First, treatment differentials will be discussed for the different subcultural groups considered earlier. We will conclude by looking at non-Western treatments for mental disorder.

Treatment differentials

Persons from ethnic minorities and from the lower social classes are less likely to utilise mental health services (e.g. Sue et al. 1991). If they do seek help, they are more likely to see junior doctors, receive somatic therapy rather than psychotherapy (e.g. Littlewood & Cross 1980) and be placed in locked wards (Bolton 1984). Responsiveness to different treatments also varies; Asians, for example, are slower to metabolise some antidepressants and faster to metabolise others (Flaskerud 2000). An entire field of research, known as **pharmacogenetics**, is devoted to the study of ethnic differences in response to drug treatments. Hence for each group, it is useful to consider not only what is typically offered by way of treatment, but also what appears to suit each group. Fernando (1995) has provided a summary of the research findings, given in Box 4.3.

Dropout rates are also influenced by **cultural responsiveness factors** – whether the therapist and client share culture and language. Sue et al. (1991) found in a large-scale study that **matching by ethnicity** was associated with lower dropout rates and more treatment sessions for Asians and Mexicans (though not for African Americans). Language match was also beneficial.

These points indicate that it should be possible to develop services for the treatment of mental disorder that take more account of cultural variability than those that exist at the present time.

Client-centred treatment has been advocated in order to address some of the concerns raised in this chapter. The aim is to provide treatment appropriate to the cultural identity of the client. Sue (2000) suggested that working with clients in this way should involve the steps outlined in Box 4.3. Such treatment will also require the increased training of minority-group therapists, or therapists who are specialised in working with minority groups (Lopez et al. 1989). This can be regarded as part of a general need to develop services that display **cultural sensitivity** (Sue 1988). According to Sue (2000) the key requirements for such a system are:

- parallel services for different ethnic groups;
- fit of characteristics (training more ethnic providers);
- cognitive fit (matching therapists to clients carefully);
- provision of guidelines for culturally competent care at the level

of the provider (therapist), agency (organisation) and systems (political level).

BOX 4.3 Culture and assessment of clients

- Self-assessment by clinician of ethnocentric biases.
- Assessment of client's culture and experience.
- Assessment of own knowledge of the client's background (especially deficiencies in that knowledge).
- Pre-therapy intervention (explanation of process to client).
- Hypothesise and test hypotheses.
- Attend to credibility and giving.
- Understand the nature of discomfort and resistances from the client's perspective.
- Develop a strategy for intervention.
- Address (un)willingness of clients to consult.
- Educate the community at large about issues involved.

Non-Western treatments

In other cultures, a variety of treatments exist for mental disorder that differ from those available in Western cultures. In some countries, such as China, they operate alongside the institutional treatments based on the Western model of psychiatry.

Forms of treatment

In non-Western cultures, folk healers (e.g. shamans, curanderos) generally deal with mental disorder by becoming possessed by spirits during a trance. In this state they can master the spirits, and exorcise or neutralise the spirits that possess others. Also important in folk healing is **symbolic healing**, which is the use of accepted symbols such as herbs, rituals and chants, to transform experience and provide understanding of the problem.

South Asian shamanism considers mental disorder to be the result of possession by ghosts and demons. The shaman, employing rituals, aims to become possessed by powerful gods with enough status to banish them. The patient also has a trance state induced, so that the shaman can converse with the demon directly and encourage or force it to depart. Symbols used include recitation of mantras (sacred verses), costume props for the shaman to assist with taking on the form of a particular god, offerings to the spirits or ritual burnings (e.g. of hair clippings) to symbolise the removal of the demon. The patient is highly suggestible while in the trance state, and this encourages an **existential shift** (change in the way in which the mental disorder is conceptualised and experienced) (Obeyesekere 1977).

A curandero may treat susto in South America by having an initial diagnostic session with the client to identify the cause of the initial episode, which will be agreed with the client. Then there will be a healing session, in which the soul is coaxed back into the patient's body by massage and sweating treatments (Rubel 1977).

Other cultures may also employ different forms of medicine from those used in the West, such as Ayurvedic medicine (Asia), Chinese medicine, Yoruban (Africa) and Tibetan medicine. Generally, they do not view the mind and body as separate, and treatment is given for both. This may involve herbs, rituals or acupuncture.

Are the treatments effective?

That these may be effective is acknowledged by Prince (1964), who reported a case of severe neurosis that had not responded to 4 years of both Western and non-Western treatment. The patient was eventually cured by a Yoruba healer using sacrifice and ritual. Prince concluded that 'Western psychiatric techniques are not in my opinion demonstrably superior to many indigenous Yoruba practices' (Fernando 1988, p. 161). Similarly, Finkler (1981) found that spiritualism in rural Mexico was helpful in the treatment of neuroses.

Further support comes from the finding (Sartorius et al. 1986) that schizophrenics do better in less developed countries than in Britain, America and Denmark. They found that 25% of schizophrenic patients fell into the best two outcome categories in developed countries, compared to 39% in less developed countries. In developed countries 65% fell into the worst two categories, compared to 38% in the less developed countries.

How do the treatments work?

Treatment of mental disorder in the West is based on a view of disorder that is focused on the individual. In other cultures, the disorder is viewed as a social problem that involves the community at large – what Kleinman (1980) refers to as **cultural healing**. This aims to resolve conflicts, reintegrate the individual and restore the cohesion of the group. Sorcery, such as the casting of spells or curses for example, may be blamed for the disorder, but may in itself be the result of social conflict that needs to be addressed. Thus group ties are strengthened by treatment, unlike the situation in the West.

Murphy (1964) notes that the shaman is psychotherapeutic because he reinforces the shared beliefs of the group, involves both the individual and the community in treatment, shows a personal ability to master spirits, identifies the source of the illness (e.g. breaching a taboo) and prescribes acts that will remedy the problem.

The positive outcomes have also been attributed to the level of **expressed emotion** shown by the families of patients in the different countries. This is the amount of criticism and hostility shown (Brown et al. 1962) and has been shown to lead to re-admission in Western patients who have been discharged from hospital. In other cultures, such as India (23%), it is found to be lower than in Britain (48%) (Karno et al. 1987).

Another explanation is in terms of modern versus premodern **meaning systems** (Castillo 1995). In premodern meaning systems, symptom causes are located externally to the individual (e.g. possession by an outside force). Modern meaning systems locate the causes internally, in the form of illness, relieving the individual of responsibility (Waxler 1979).

Antonovsky (1979) refers to the concept of **coherence** in healing. This is the idea that the environment (internal and external) is predictable and can be controlled, providing hope for the future. The three components of coherence are:

- Comprehensibility (the understanding of the source and mechanism of the problem; this will differ according to culture, and may refer to a disease process, as in the medical model, or a spirit attack).
- Manageability (feeling that the situation is not out of control, and can be treated whether by rituals or drugs).

- Meaningfulness (providing a sense of purpose to the experience, such as a religious meaning; the medical model is poor in this respect).

According to Dow (1986) this amounts to inducing an existential shift. This means changing the way the problem is conceptualised and experienced, which then provides opportunities for change. If the therapist and client share cultural schemas related to the problem, there will be better understanding and more change.

Conclusion

It is clear from the research considered in this chapter that 'we have failed to see others clearly but have instead treated their cultural worlds like funhouse mirrors that hold up distorted reflections of our own cultural preoccupations' (Kirmayer & Minas 2000, p. 439).

As Fernando (1988) makes clear, all psychiatries have a common purpose in different cultures – to maintain the mental health of individuals. This, rather than the maintenance of any particular system of psychiatry, must be the focus for the future.

Chapter summary

In this chapter we have taken a wide-ranging perspective on the influence of culture and subculture on mental disorder. In the first section, we have seen how cultural meaning systems affect the ways that different cultures view behaviour. The role of transcultural psychiatry in exploring the effects this has on mental disorder has been outlined in terms of absolutism, universality and cultural relativism. Cultural differences in response to unusual behaviours demonstrate that in non-Western cultures behaviours such as hallucinations are not recognised as problems. Different cultures also show differences in the prevalence of and mode of expression of disorders. Within a culture, too, there are marked differences between subcultural groups. The ultimate expression of these differences in disorders is in culture-bound syndromes, found in some cultures but not elsewhere. Different cultural groups also have different ways of treating mental disorder, and within a culture they may receive differential treatment. It is concluded that there is a need to ensure culture-appropriate treatment for all.

Draw up a table to show how different cultures and subcultures differ in response to schizophrenic behaviours, rates of occurrence of schizophrenia and the treatment of schizophrenia.

Repeat the exercise for other categories of mental disorder, such as depression.

Review exercise

Further reading

Fernando, S. (1988) *Race and Culture in Psychiatry*. London: Croom Helm. (Still the most thorough and easily read text on racial issues.)

Pilgrim, D. & Rogers, A. (1999) *A Sociology of Mental Health and Illness*. Buckingham, UK: Open University Press. (Although a sociological text primarily, this gives clear and thorough coverage of the subcultural issues.)

Russell, D. (1995). *Women, Madness and Medicine*. London: Polity. (Easy to read, good detail of women's issues.)

5

Conclusion: synoptic issues and debates

This book deals with a wide range of issues pertinent to the classification and diagnosis of mental disorder. In this chapter we will be summarising what has been said and looking at the main implications of these issues.

In the first chapter, we have seen that defining abnormal behaviour is problematic. By exploring a wide range of criteria, from legal to psychosocial, we have demonstrated the difficulties of trying to find a definition that is broad enough to cover all cases in all cultures, and yet specific enough to provide clear guidelines for practitioners. This exemplifies the **nomothetic–idiographic** debate that permeates psychology. A nomothetic approach to the study of behaviour suggests that, in line with traditional scientific thinking, it is better to study large numbers of people and produce universal laws that can be generalised. The idiographic approach is to examine each unique case in detail in order to produce an in-depth analysis of that person; this would not necessarily apply to any other individuals.

We have also looked at different models of mental disorder, which represent the variety of approaches within psychology. These range from a medical approach involving a universal classification system based on syndromes and symptoms, to a humanistic approach that places the emphasis on the individual and rejects the concept of mental illness. The practical and ethical implications of choices about definitions and models can be clearly seen when looking at the potential effects on the individuals concerned, from involuntary hospitalisation to social labelling and stigmatisation. This then provides the basis for the ethical dilemma of how best to deal with mental disorder, which is developed in the rest of the text; both the problem, and its consequences, are wide-ranging. In the words of Thomas Szasz (1960, p. 190): 'The practice of medicine is intimately tied to ethics; and the first thing that we must do, it seems to me, is to try and make this clear and explicit.'

In the second chapter, we have explored the classification systems DSM IV and ICD 10, outlining the major categories of mental disorder included and the procedures through which a diagnosis is arrived at. To be considered scientific, these systems have to be shown to be both reliable and valid. Research has shown, however, that the reliability and validity of both the systems and the procedures on which they rely can be questioned. Clearly, if the systems do not relate to separate syndromes with different implications for treatment (validity) and if clinicians cannot use them to arrive at the same judgement for the same individual (reliability), they are not performing adequately. The question then becomes whether the systems simply need further adjustment, or whether the whole process is misguided.

Furthermore, many psychologists feel that the medical model (on which the classification systems are based) is not an appropriate one for clinicians to subscribe to. They reject the idea of reductionist explanations for mental disorder, based on physiological functioning and animal research, and argue that this in turn makes the current psychiatric classification systems redundant. This has led some writers (e.g. Pilgrim 2000) to urge that psychologists should reject the diagnostic systems in favour of an individual analysis of each client's behaviour problems. This should be based on the experience and social context of that client and expressed in everyday language. As such, it would be more useful in planning treatment and would avoid many of the difficulties just outlined. To quote Pilgrim (2000, p. 304): 'we should be in the business of understanding psychological difference, not reducing experiential and behavioural variations to fixed pre-emptive constructs supplied by professionals.'

The third chapter focuses on one particular syndrome identified in the current classification systems. MPD (or DID) has been explored in terms of historical and geographic changes in the extent to which it has been evident. The favoured explanation for the problem, in terms of a personal history of childhood abuse, has also been carefully examined. The major debate raised was whether MPD could be seen as spontaneous or iatrogenic – in other words, whether it is genuine or the result of clinical bias. It was concluded that neither view gives a sufficient explanation of the evidence available. The recent 'epidemic' of MPD in certain countries has been linked with the views of clinicians in those countries, and with the social conditions that might have provoked those views. Associated development of interest in child abuse and involvement of the mass media in everyday life may have led both clinicians and members of the public to jointly develop a social construction of MPD as a form of mental disorder. Thus both clinicians and clients are swayed by the social context, leading clinicians to be extra vigilant for cases of MPD, and clients to see it as an acceptable way of expressing their distress. The diagnostic system, then, is not solely responsible for describing what is observed, but is itself a socially constructed product.

In the case of MPD, there are further implications in terms of free will and determinism. For example, as seen in the discussion about the legal aspects of MPD, it is difficult to decide whether such individuals are responsible for their behaviour while in altered states. The ethical consequences for the individual of these social constructions, then, are potentially crucial. To quote Acocella (1999, p. 138): 'The question about MPD should not be whether the diagnosis is real but whether it is helpful. It is not.'

Chapter 4 deals with cultural and subcultural variation in mental disorder, and what this means for the way that it is diagnosed and treated in the Western cultures. Supporting the idea of social constructionism, as well as the problems of definition outlined in the first chapter, we have seen that different behaviours may be recognised as abnormal in different cultures, and that disorders may be expressed in different ways in different cultures. Differences may extend still further, with certain cultural conditions being implicated in the causation of mental disorder. There may be some disorders that are found in some cultures and not in others, which raises arguments about the involvement of nature versus nurture. If nature is predominant, it could be argued that such differences are genetically caused; if nurture is considered, different experiences may be the cause. Whether these are in fact distinct syndromes or just variations on those that exist elsewhere is difficult to determine.

Whatever the explanation, the existence of such cultural variation weakens the case for a universal system for classifying mental disorder. It also strengthens the emphasis on an idiographic approach, in the sense that people from different cultural backgrounds may require different treatment. Western psychiatry may need to be replaced by a transcultural approach; there is also scope to argue for a transcultural psychology that takes account of cultural variation and is less focused on western lifestyles.

Fernando(1995) discusses a multi-systemic assessment that is based on an analysis of the individual's problems on a variety of levels (looking at family, community and spiritual/religious aspects, for example). This in turn results in multiple interventions tailored to the specific nature of the problem and the individual's specific cultural background. He concludes: 'by careful and sensitive training and practice, mental health care can be rendered appropriate for the need of those who require it, can be just and fair to all sections of the community, and can make contact with real problems of real people' (p. 215).

That, at any rate, is indisputable.

6

Study aids

Improving your essay-writing skills
Sample essays and examiner's comments
Summaries of key research papers

Improving your essay-writing skills

At this point in the book you have acquired the knowledge necessary to tackle the exam itself. Answering exam questions is a skill that this chapter shows you how to improve. Examiners obviously have first-hand knowledge about what goes wrong in exams. For example, candidates frequently do not answer the question that has been set – rather they answer the one that they hoped would come up, or they do not make effective use of the knowledge they have, but just 'dump their psychology' on the page and hope the examiner will sort it out for them. A grade C answer usually contains appropriate material but tends to be limited in detail and commentary. To lift such an answer to a grade A or B may require no more than a little more detail, better use of material and coherent organisation. It is important to appreciate that it may not involve writing at any greater length, but might even necessitate the elimination of passages that do not add to the quality of the answer and some elaboration of those that do.

By studying the essays presented in this chapter and the examiner's comments, you can learn how to turn your grade C answer into a grade

A. Typically it only involves an extra 6 marks out of 30. Please note that marks given by the examiner in the practice essays should be used as a guide only and are not definitive. They represent the 'raw' marks that would be likely to be given to answers to AQA(A) questions. In the AQA(A) examination, an examiner would award a maximum of 12 marks for knowledge and understanding (called Assessment Objective 1 – AO1) and 12 marks for evaluation, analysis and commentary (Assessment Objective 2 – AO2). In this part of the specification you are also assessed on your ability to be synoptic. Synopticity involves demonstrating a breadth of knowledge and evaluation of a broad range of psychological perspectives and methodologies. In order to maximise your marks you must ensure that you address such issues.

The details of this marking scheme are given in Appendix C of Paul Humphreys' titles *Exam Success in AQA(A) Psychology* in this series, *Exam Success in AEB Psychology* and the forthcoming title *Exam Success in AQA(A) Psychology*. Remember that these are the raw marks and not the same as those given on the examination certificate received ultimately by the candidate, because all examining boards are required to use a common standardised system, the Uniform Mark Scale (UMS), which adjusts all raw scores to a single standard across all boards.

The essays given here are notionally written by an 18-year-old in 45 minutes and marked bearing that in mind. It is important when writing to such a tight time limit that you make every sentence count. Each essay in this chapter is followed by detailed comments about its strengths and weaknesses. The most common problems to watch out for are:

- Failure to answer the question but reproducing a model answer to a similar question that you have pre-learned.
- Not delivering the right balance between description and evaluation/ analysis. Remember they are always weighted 50/50.
- Writing 'everything you know' about a topic in the hope that something will get credit and the examiner will sort your work out for you. Remember that excellence demands selectivity, so improvements can often be made by removing material that is irrelevant to the question set and elaborating material that is relevant.
- Failing to use your material effectively. It is not enough to place the information on the page – you must also show the examiner that you are using it to make a particular point.

For more ideas on how to write good essays you should consult *Exam Success in AEB Psychology* and the forthcoming title *Exam Success in AQA(A) Psychology* (by Paul Humphreys) in this series.

Sample essays and examiner's comments

Practice essay 1

Describe and evaluate ICD and DSM as ways of classifying abnormal behaviour. (30 marks) [AQA 2000]

Starting point: 'Describe' is an Assessment Objective One term which requires candidates to present evidence of their knowledge of the two classification systems named in the question. This could include identifying the structure of the classification system (e.g. the axes used in DSM) and the major categories of disorder. Diagnostic criteria and examples could be provided. 'Evaluate' is an Assessment Objective Two term that requires the candidates to assess the value of the systems. This could be done through comparison of the two approaches with one another and with earlier systems, and through a discussion of their reliability and validity. Ethical and practical implications could also be considered. Synopticity (i.e. the ability to show an appreciation of a wide range of viewpoints on the issue concerned) is assessed in both AO1 and AO2. This can be explored by a consideration of issues (in this case, gender and cultural bias, and ethics) and debates (which could include free will and determinism, reductionism and psychology as a science).

Candidate's answer

ICD 10 was introduced in 1992/3 and is an updated version of ICD 9. It is published by the World Health Organisation (WHO). It identifies 11 categories of mental disorder. These include schizophrenia, mood disorders, adult personality and behaviour disorders, mental retardation, childhood/adolescent emotional disorders, organic disorders and neurotic disorders. For example, in the schizophrenia category are listed the different types of schizophrenia – simple, hebephrenic, catatonic and paranoid, along with 'undifferentiated', residual and other types of schizotypal disorder.

In the neurotic, stress-related and somatoform disorders category are phobias, anxiety disorders, OCD and multiple personality disorder. The mood disorders category (also known as affective disorders) includes bipolar affective diorder and recurrent depressive disorder. The eating disorders anorexia nervosa and bulimia nervosa are classified as behavioural syndromes associated with physiological disturbances and physical factors.

DSM IV was introduced in 1994 and is published by the American Psychiatric Association (APA). It is an updated version of DSM IIIR. It has 17 major categories (as noted ICD 10 has only 11). These include schizophrenic and other psychotic disorders, anxiety disorders, eating disorders and mood disorders. Other categories are dissociative disorders, somatoform disorders, adjustment disorders, personality disorders and sexual and gender identity disorders. Included as sexual and gender identity disorders are sexual desire disorders and paraphilias (such as fetishism) as well as gender identity disorders.

Although ICD and DSM are similar, they differ in a number of ways. For example, neurotic, stress-related and somatoform disorders is a single category in ICD whereas in DSM IV the disorders covered appear under separate headings. However, sometimes the reverse is true, and one category in DSM includes two or more categories in ICD. It is this that accounts for the fact that there are different numbers of categories in the two systems (11 in ICD and 17 in DSM).

Also, the systems differ in terms of whether they use the words 'neurosis' and 'psychosis'. Traditionally, these have been seen as very different disorders, but in both ICD 10 and DSM IV the distinction between them is not made. However, DSM IV still uses the word 'psychotic', which ICD 10 does not, whereas ICD 10 uses the word 'neurotic', which is not used in DSM IV. Neither of the systems uses the word 'mental illness' any more.

There are many problems associated with both ICD and DSM. These are both practical and ethical. The practical problems are the most important, and include reliability and validity. Reliability refers to the consistency of measurement. In psychology, this means that would the same person be diagnosed in the same way by one psychiatrist on two different occasions (test–retest reliability)?

Several studies (Cooper?) have shown that British and American psychiatrists diagnose differently. A diagnosis of schizophrenia is more likely in Britain than in America, but for manic depression the reverse is true. This, then, suggests that diagnosis is not reliable. If it is not reliable then it cannot be valid (Cardwell).

Rosenhan conducted a famous study in which perfectly normal people attempted to gain entry to psychiatric hospitals, complaining of hearing words like 'empty', 'hollow' and 'thud'. When they gained admission (all did) they started behaving normally. One man started writing notes about his experiences. Their normal behaviour was taken as being a further sign of their diagnosis (schizophrenia) but the point is that they fooled the psychiatrists in the first place. The man's writing behaviour was recorded as 'patient engaged in writing'.

Examiner's comments

This is a well-constructed essay that has a good degree of focus on the question set. The first part of the essay is almost entirely descriptive, and gives a reasonably detailed outline of the main categories of mental disorder in the two systems. The focus is primarily on listing disorders, which has some synopticity in breadth, but more could be added by incorporating other ways of describing the schemes. What is lacking is any mention of the different axes of assessment in the DSM system, and examples of diagnostic criteria for some of the disorders. The system could also be linked to the medical model, and cultural variation could be mentioned. The AO1 mark is therefore most likely to be around the bottom of band 4 (10 marks), since it is slightly limited in both description and synopticity.

The second part of the essay deals with the evaluation (AO2). There are some good points of comparison between the two systems. The remainder of the evaluation could usefully be set in the context of the principles of science (which would introduce some synopticity) but the candidate does not mention these. There is an attempt to deal with the issue of reliability, which is quite well explained. Research evidence is somewhat lacking, however, and validity is not addressed in detail. The Rosenhan study is not really very well explained, nor is it linked to the question set in any coherent way (i.e. it is not used effectively). The study itself is not without flaws (see Chapter 2 and article 1 in the present chapter), and pre-dates the classification systems under consideration. The candidate could do a great deal here to increase the scope of the evaluation and enhance synopticity by incorporating material relating to cultural issues (Chapter 4) and social constructionism (Chapter 3). Both of these issues demonstrate that a universal classification for all eras and all places may not be achievable. A broad perspective could further be shown by looking outside the medical model at approaches such as the socio-cultural and humanistic, which place less emphasis on diagnosis and classification, and are less reductionist in their approach to behaviour. Finally, the candidate has mentioned ethical issues but failed to elaborate on them any further. The legal and personal implications of being diagnosed as having a mental disorder, or having one disorder rather than another, are considerable, and warrant development in this context. Free will and determinism is a key issue here. Hence AO2 is more likely to be around the bottom of band 3 (a mark of about 7) – reasonable, limited, with some elaboration.

Overall, this esssay would receive a mark of around 17/30, placing it on the borderline between a 'C' and a 'B' grade. To move in the direction of the 'B' grade, the candidate, who has shown quite good ability to learn facts, needs to work on evaluative skills and develop the synoptic content of essays.

Practice essay 2

(a) Outline two or more culture-bound syndromes. (10 AO1 marks)

(b) Discuss the problems raised by culture-bound syndromes for the classification and diagnosis of psychological abnormality. (5 marks AO1 + 15 marks AO2)

Starting point: 'Describe' is an AO1 term requiring candidates to present evidence of their knowledge of culture-bound syndromes. This could include symptoms, who is affected, and where the disorders are found. Case studies could also be presented here.

'Discuss' is a term that requires the candidate to both describe and evaluate the importance of culture-bound syndromes to this subject. For AO1, the candidate needs to demonstrate knowledge about the problems raised by culture-bound syndromes and about the classification and diagnostic systems in use for mental disorder. The key issue is universalism versus relativism of the systems. Synopticity can be achieved by breadth of perspective–acknowledgement that there is more than one classification system, for example. For AO2, the candidate needs to weigh up the arguments for the two sides. This can include commenting on the validity of the culture-bound syndromes themselves, and suggesting implications for clients, as well as how the problems may be resolved. Ethical and scientific issues can be introduced by way of addressing the synopticity requirement.

Candidate's answer

(a) Many people at some point in their lives will suffer from a psychological abnormality of some sort or another, e.g. depression or phobia. Some abnormalities are quite common, in fact. Psychological abnormality is another name for mental disorder, also known as mental illness. The system used for classifying mental disorder is called DSM IV. There is another known as ICD 10. Both of them are based on the medical approach, used by psychiatrists. In both of them, mental disorders are put into categories depending on the symptoms shown by patients. Schizophrenics, for example, show hallucinations, thought disorders, delusions and emotional disorders. However, schizophrenia is not considered to be an illness in all cultures. Studies have shown that there are places in Africa where hallucinations are regarded as normal behaviour. Not many non-Western countries have anorexia, a disorder where patients refuse to eat and can die eventually because they have lost too much weight. There are also other countries that have mental disorders that are not mentioned in DSM. These are called culture-bound syndromes, because they are only found in certain places in the world, like China, Asia and South America. DSM defines them as problems with behaviour or experience that are 'locality specific'.

One of these is amok, where people feel they are being picked on and become depressed. They then get violent and can attack and even kill people before they tire themselves out. Afterwards, they forget all about the things they have done. This is found in parts of Asia, and only seems to occur in men.

Another example is ataque de nervios, which is found in women in Latin America. They become very frightened, seen as anxiety, shortness of breath, crying, shaking and fainting. It often occurs after the death of a member of the family, and they may try to commit suicide. Dhat syndrome, on the other hand, is found in men in India. They become anxious and depressed because they have too much sex, which they think makes them weak and tired. In koro, a Chinese mental disorder, the person thinks that the penis is disappearing back into the body and they will die as a result. This makes them very anxious and likely to faint. Women can get this too, their main symptom being that they think their breasts are disappearing. Another disorder, called taijin, is found mostly in Japan. This is where patients think that they smell awful and will not socialise because of this. They may refuse to leave the house altogether, rather like some phobics.

(b) There are a lot of these disorders, and they are listed in the back of DSM IV, the manual that lists all mental disorders. The problem with them is that psychologists who work in these countries will not know how to diagnose and treat them, because there is not much information about them in DSM, which is based on American mental disorders. There are also a lot of others that DSM does not mention. McCajor Hall mentions 36, whereas DSM has just 25. We could extend DSM to include them as separate disorders, but this has not been done yet. The problem with this is that they may really be the same as the ones that we already know about, but they just have different names, or show themselves in slightly different ways. The Japanese disorder where they avoid other people (taijin) seems a bit like social phobia, for example.

Psychologists argue about whether these disorders are really different to ours or not. Some psychologists, such as Kiev, think that our mental disorders apply to all cultures, and that culture-bound syndromes do not really exist. This is called universalism. Others think that there are differences, known as relativism. These may be the result of different behaviours being acceptable and unacceptable in a particular society, differences in diagnosis or help-seeking, or perhaps genetic differences. Whatever the reason, it probably is not right to assume that everybody is the same as us, because if they are different they should get different treatment. According to Fernando, their own ways of treating things (using rituals, for example) are sometimes more successful than ours.

Until there is more research into culture-bound syndromes we cannot really decide one way or the other what to do about them. It is important to decide in the first place whether they are genuine disorders or not. Ataque de nervios has been found by Canino to be quite common and accepted in the places where it is seen, but according to Marano, windigo (a disorder claimed to exist in North American Indians) does not really exist at all. The problem is that it is not easy to do the research when you do not speak the language or understand the background that people come from. They see things differently to us. A lot of people in other countries may not go to see a psychologist when they have problems, so they will not be included in any research studies anyway. They may prefer to go and see someone else, like a doctor or a shaman. For example, Rack found that in Asia, people with depression would go to their doctor and complain about physical symptoms rather than mental ones.

However, it would be wrong to suggest that the current system is perfect. There is still a great need for cultural illnesses to be discovered and diagnosed properly in order to give mentally ill people in all cultures the chance to be diagnosed and treated. They deserve to be given as much help as people in our society. This is why DSM now contains guidelines for psychologists in our society who have to deal with people from other cultures.

Examiner's comments

Like the previous example, this essay is also quite well constructed and has kept to the point throughout. There is a good balance of description and evaluation of the problems, although the answer generally suffers from a lack of detail and research evidence. Quite a lot of points are being made, although in many cases they are simply stated and not elaborated on to any great extent. In that sense, there is more breadth than depth in the essay.

In part (a) the candidate has given some accurate if brief examples of culture-bound syndromes. As this part of the essay is limited but reasonably detailed, a mark of around 5 out of 10 would be appropriate. This could be improved by providing more detailed descriptions and some case studies. Concentrating on a smaller number of syndromes, and providing more detail, may well have been a better use of the candidate's time.

Part (b) is rather short by comparison, given that it carries more marks than part (a). As regards AO1 (description) the candidate has given a brief account of how DSM operates. The basic issues of relativism and universalism have been outlined. The candidate could improve on this by giving an account of the DSM axes and the place of culture-bound syndromes in DSM. Synoptically, it could be acknowledged that there is another classification system (ICD) and that both are derived from the medical model. A distinction between practical and ethical implications of cultural differences could also be made, with perhaps an acknowledgement that problems facing immigrant and minority groups in Western societies may be just as great, if not greater, then those facing people in other parts of the world. For this part of the question, the AO1 mark would be 3/5.

For AO2, the points made are good ones, but could be elaborated on and explained rather more than they have been here. The need for research, for example, can be explained more fully with respect to the scientific principles involved and issues such as reliability and validity. Explanations for the syndromes could also be considered in more depth, giving an opportunity for synopticity when drawing on different perspectives such as the biological and social constructionist. The research that does exist (see Chapter 4) could be included and evaluated in turn. Critical commentary on DSM could be extended (perhaps with reference to material from Chapter 2). A mark of 8/15 would be suitable here for AO2 – reasonable, limited, with some elaboration and commentary.

Overall, the essay would receive a mark of around 16, which would be a grade C. This candidate needs to work on more detailed knowledge of the topic, and greater elaboration of what is already known. More explanation of many of the points made, references to research, and more synoptic assessment, could have raised this essay to a B grade.

Summaries of key research papers

In this section we will be looking at short summaries of three research papers that have been referred to in the course of this book. The section includes one study from each of the three main chapters (2–4), which relate in turn to the main sections of the AQA specification for this area. You may find it helpful to make a very brief summary of your own for each, including just one or two key points and a note about which of the areas covered in the book the study is most relevant to. Remember that comments about ethics theoretical perspectives and methodology can form a useful part of your synoptic assessment.

Article 1

On being sane in insane places

D. Rosenhan (1973). *Science*, *179*, 250–8.

Notes

This study never fails to make a powerful impression on those who read it, but it is nevertheless often misconstrued. It tells us very little about the reliability and validity of the *current* classification system for mental disorder. Ethically, it can be criticised for employing deception, in that the pseudopatients were faking symptoms and asking to be admitted to the hospital concerned. What it *does* show is that clinicians can be deceived and that normality is not easily detectable. Further, it demonstrates that labels, once applied, are both difficult to shake off and capable of influencing the behaviour of others towards the labelled individual. As you read the study, think carefully about the ethical issues it raises.

Summary

Eight sane pseudopatients (including Rosenhan) gained admission to 12 different psychiatric hospitals on the basis that they were hearing voices saying 'empty', 'hollow' and 'thud'. In all other respects they gave accurate information about themselves to admissions staff, and asked to be admitted to the hospital. After admission, they behaved normally, with a view to being discharged as soon as possible.

They were admitted (in all cases but one) with a diagnosis of schiz-ophrenia, and spent 7–52 days in hospital (average stay 19 days). The nurses reported that they showed no signs of abnormality, and the 35/118 other patients were suspicious of their status as 'real' patients. Case notes prepared for some of the patients, as well as interpretations of current behaviours, demonstrated that behaviours that might otherwise be considered 'normal' were in this context being interpreted in terms of pathology. Pacing the corridors, for example, was associated with nervousness rather than boredom, and waiting for the canteen to open as oral-acquisitive behaviour. Responses to attempts by pseudo-patients to initiate contact with staff (approaching and asking a question) were compared with those obtained on a university campus.

Table 6.1 Response of psychiatric and campus staff to attempts at initiating contact

Response (%)	Psychiatrists	Campus staff	University physicians
Moves on, head averted	71	0	0
Stops and talks	4	100	90

The results showed that failure to respond to questions, and moving on with head averted were more common by far in the hospital setting (see Table 6.1). Note that university physicians were less responsive when the question asked was about how to find a psychiatrist. This was interpreted in terms of the powerlessness and depersonalisation that results from the application of a psychiatric label. The discharge of the pseudopatients with a diagnosis of 'schizophrenia in remission' shows that the label itself is difficult to shake off once applied.

Rosenhan was also interested in whether the insane might be judged sane – the reverse of the first demonstration. Staff at a teaching hospital, familiar with the earlier study, were told to expect a pseudopatient to arrive at the hospital during a 3-month period. Every patient who arrived was to be rated on a 10-point scale to indicate the likelihood that she or he was a pseudopatient. Although all 193 patients seen were in fact supposed to be genuine, 23 were suspected of being pseudopatients by at least one psychiatrist and 41 by at least one staff member. Rosenhan pointed out that this reversal could have occurred because the staff had shifted their standards, feeling that their diagnostic prowess was being put to the test. Clearly, it challenges the idea that clinicians use clear-cut, objective criteria as the basis for diagnosis. As Gross (1994) comments in his summary of the paper: 'any diagnostic process which lends itself so readily to massive errors of this sort cannot be a very reliable one. ' This in turn means that it cannot be valid.

Article 2

Functional magnetic resonance imaging of personality switches in a woman with Dissociative Identity Disorder

G. Tsai, D. Condie, M-T. Wu and I-W. Chang (1999).
Harvard Review of Psychiatry, 7, 119.

Notes

This article is about a case study of an MPD patient. As such, it may not be possible to generalise the findings to other MPD patients. However, it makes important links between activity in the brain, particularly the areas of the brain responsible for memories, and the personality switching that may occur in this syndrome. There are very few physiological studies of such patients, and any evidence for a biological basis to the disorder represents a considerable contribution. Whether the physiological differences noted are in fact a cause or an effect of the disorder also remains to be seen.

Summary

The 33-year-old patient, known as Marnie, was originally treated for depression. After her mother died, she demonstrated to the staff treating her a different personality, whom she called Mimi. In complete contrast to Marnie, Mimi was lively and optimistic, and revealed that she had been beaten, as well as sexually and psychologically abused by her alcoholic mother. A male personality had emerged as well, who had the job of inflicting bruises on Marnie so that the mother would be deceived into thinking that she had already beaten her. There was also a personality called Guardian, an 8-year-old girl who had the job of looking after Marnie when her mother was mistreating her.

Studies of Marnie used an fMRI. This is the most sophisticated brain-imaging device currently available, which can analyse the extent to which different areas of the brain are showing changes in blood flow, and thus highlight any increase in activity. The studies revealed that her hippocampus was shrunken to less than half the normal size. During her years of therapy, Marnie had developed the ability to shift personalities at the request of her therapist. Therefore the researchers decided to investigate the functioning of her brain while this was occurring. She was asked to press a button to signal when Guardian took over, and when Marnie returned. As a control, she was asked to imagine being taken over by an 8-year-old fake alter called 'Player'.

The major change observed was that as Guardian took over, activity was reduced in the hippocampus and the surrounding region of the temporal cortex. When Marnie returned, activity in the right side of the hippocampus increased again. These changes were not observed when 'Player' was imagined to be taking over. The researchers concluded that MPD is the result of a form of damage to the brain resulting from excessive, repeated stress in early childhood. Patients suffering from post-traumatic stress disorder also have shrunken hippocampuses, supporting this idea. The mechanism may be the production of glucocorticoids, as part of the response to stress. These have been shown to be toxic to the hippocampus, and capable of inducing cell death in that area. It is suggested that in those who are vulnerable, such a shrinkage may lead to poor memory, and also to difficulty with recall of memories that are formed when in a particular emotional state. As the individual's feelings of identity are dependent on memories, these too become disrupted, leading to MPD.

Article 3

A case of koro in a 20-year-old Irish male
J. Tobin (1996). *Irish Journal of Psychological Medicine*, *13*(2), 72–73.

Notes

Koro is listed in the appendix to DSM IV as a culture-bound syndrome, indicating that it is a disorder that is only found in certain geographical areas. The finding of a case such as the one documented here, in an area where it is not generally known, raises doubts about the assumption that it is a genuine culture-bound syndrome. If it is not, then possibly the others are also suspect, and the case for universalism is supported. However, it is still difficult to explain why there are differences in the rates of occurrence in different areas or cultures.

Other cases are also outlined here that meet some, but not all, of the criteria for koro. This is important in the context of the argument about whether or not the listed culture-bound syndromes are in fact distinct syndromes. Indeed, the major syndromes on Axes I and II of DSM IV can also be criticised on the grounds that it is not always easy to decide which criteria are essential. Are people who only display some of the symptoms free of mental disorder?

Summary

The name koro means 'head of turtle', and refers to a culture-bound syndrome thought to occur only in China and Indonesia. The case reported was of a 20-year-old single Irish male. He showed the three essential symptoms of koro, these being:

- a belief that the genitals are shrinking;
- a belief that they will shrink back into the abdomen;
- a belief that this will result in death.

As a consequence of these beliefs, he had tied a lead fishing line to his genitals to prevent them from disappearing into his abdomen. Chinese patients use penile clamps that are specially made for the purpose, indicating the extent to which the disorder is recognised in that country.

Non-Chinese patients have been reported before. In 1984 Berrios and Morley reviewed 15 cases that had been reported in the literature, but only two of these fulfilled all three criteria. In 1992, Heyman and Fahy reported the symptoms of koro in a man who also suffered from HIV and depression.

The disorder is often reported in association with severe anxiety or psychotic/affective illness. The Irish case had no previous history of psychiatric disorder, but presented with impotence. He displayed extreme agitation, and was unable to remain still. His background was impoverished, and he was unemployed, with a child to support. As a result of his girlfriend's expectations that he would provide for the child, he reported experiencing stress.

However, the family background was clearly pathological. His father suffered from a schizoaffective disorder, and his mother had reactive depression. Four brothers, also living in the family home, had a variety of problems. The most problematic of them suffered from learning difficulties and manic depression, and had made numerous suicide attempts. Two others were twins; one suffered from schizophrenia, while the other had endogenous depression and a sexual identity disorder. The fourth brother was psychotic. The home environment was associated with high levels of expressed emotion, mostly resulting from the problems of the suicidal brother.

The details of the case indicate that a genetic predisposition to psychosis, stress and an emotional, impoverished family environment may all have contributed to the disorder observed. Treatment given was in the form of the antipsychotic drug flupenthixol. This is similar to the phenthiazine drugs used to treat schizophrenia, and it was able to bring the delusions under control.

Glossary

The first occurrence of each of these words is highlighted in **bold** type in the main text. Note that mental disorders are defined in Chapter 2 and different types of culture-bound syndromes in Chapter 4.

absolutism   The view that abnormal behaviour is biologically determined and will take exactly the same form in all cultures.

aetiological validity   The idea that a diagnostic category is valid (i.e. represents a distinct syndrome) because all the cases that occur are caused by the same factors.

alter   One of the sub-personalities demonstrated by a person with multiple personality disorder.

asymmetrical amnesia   The finding that in multiple personality disorder only some of the alters are aware of events that occur when other alters are in control.

bimodal distribution   A distribution that has two modes, i.e. in which scores cluster around two distinct points in the range.

chaining   The triggering of memories of childhood abuse through hearing the recollections of others.

client-centred treatment   Treatment that is appropriate to the cultural identity of the client.

clinical assessment   The process of gathering information about a client in order to gain a better understanding of presenting problems.

clinical utility   How often a test correctly identifies that a person has a particular disorder or is clear of it.

cognitive triad   A negative view of the self, the world and the future, associated with depressive thinking by Beck.

coherence   In this context, having the confidence that the environment (internal and external) can be controlled, and problems mastered.

collectivist culture   A culture in which the group takes precedence over individuals.

comorbidity   Having more than one disorder at a time.

concurrent validity   Checking a new test by comparing results obtained with those from an established test that is already known to be valid.

construct validity   Providing evidence that a hypothetical construct can usefully explain a network of findings and may therefore be 'real'.

criterion validity   Checking a test by comparing the performance of groups that would be expected to differ.

cultural healing   Involvement of the community in the treatment of mental disorder.

cultural meaning systems   The body of knowledge that the individual acquires from the culture he or she lives in.

cultural relativism   The view that mental disorder differs in different cultures.

cultural responsiveness factors   Factors based on cultural differences that influence the rate of drop-out from treatment.

cultural sensitivity   Being aware of the needs of people from different cultures.

culture   The learned system of values, beliefs, rules and practices that is passed on from one generation to the next and shared by a large group of people.

culture-bound syndromes   Mental disorders that are found only in certain cultures.

descriptive validity   The proposal that a valid classification system should identify categories of mental disorder, which differ from one another, but are homogeneous within each category.

determinism   The idea that our behaviour is the result of factors beyond our control, including environmental, biological and unconscious influences.

diagnosis   The process of outlining the client's symptoms and matching them with the syndromes detailed in the classification system.

ethnicity A sense of belonging to a particular group, based on race, religion or culture.

ethnocentric psychiatric constructs Constructs that result from taking a biased (often Western) view of mental disorder.

existential shift A change in the way that a mental disorder (or any other aspect of life) is conceptualised and experienced.

expressed emotion In this context, the amount of criticism and hostility shown by families of patients with mental disorders.

face validity A method of assessing the validity of a measure by simply inspecting the contents of the test concerned.

factor analysis Statistical analysis of test scores that shows how many factors can account for the variability in scores of a large group of people.

false memory syndrome A reference to cases in which patients claim to have been abused as children but objective evidence to support their claims is lacking.

family therapies Therapies that focus on patterns of disturbed behaviour in families, rather than looking at the individual member who has presented with problems.

fMRI Functional Magnetic Resonance Imaging – a very sensitive technique for observing the functioning of different areas of the brain.

free will The view that we can make conscious decisions about our behaviour rather than it being determined by factors outside our control.

functional analysis A method used by behaviourally oriented therapists to ascertain the conditions responsible for maintaining behaviour, including settings, prompts and consequences.

genome lag An idea proposed by evolutionary theorists that some genes may persist in a species for a period of time after they have ceased to be useful.

hippocampus A subcortical structure embedded in the temporal lobe of the brain, which is important for laying down new memories.

hypnosis A method of inducing a trance-like state in which the individual responds to suggestions made by the hypnotist.

iatrogenic This means that the system in place for treating disorders may also in fact induce them in some cases.

idiographic An approach within psychology that focuses on a detailed understanding of the individual, rather than examining the behaviour of groups to establish general laws.

individualist culture A culture in which the individual takes priority over the group.

interrater reliability The level of consistency found in ratings (e.g. of some aspects of behaviour) given by different raters.

learned helplessness A state, associated by Seligman with depression, in which apathy results from being unable to escape from an unpleasant situation.

matching by ethnicity Pairing therapists and clients according to ethnic origins.

meaning systems In this context, cultural differences in whether mental disorders are attributed to causes that are internal or external to the individual.

mental state interview A structured interview that aims to evaluate the current functioning of the person referred for treatment.

model A system of beliefs about the causes and treatment for disorders.

nature–nurture debate The argument about the relative importance of environment and genetics in determining our behaviour.

nomothetic approach The study of large groups of people in order to discover general laws of behaviour.

normal distribution curve A symmetrical bell-shaped distribution curve in which the mean, median and mode all fall on the same point.

PET scanner A technique for assessing the functioning of the brain through the use of Positron Emission Tomography.

pharmacogenetics The study of ethnic differences in response to drug treatment.

predictive validity Checking the validity of a test by testing predictions about the performance of high and low scorers in some other respect (e.g. academic achievement of high and low IQ groups should differ if the IQ test is valid).

prevalence The proportion of the population suffering from a given disorder at a particular point in time.

projective techniques Tests of personality that ask individuals to respond to ambiguous material such as an ink blot.

psychiatric imperialism Dominating other cultural groups by taking an ethnocentric view of mental disorder.

psychometric tests   Instruments devised by psychologists to measure mental functioning.

race   Membership of a particular group of people who are biologically distinctive.

reactivity   A change in behaviour as a result of being observed.

reductionism   The suggestion that explaining behaviour on the most basic level (e.g. the biological) is superior to explanations offered at other levels (e.g. the social).

reliability   Consistency of results in an experiment or agreement between clinicians about diagnosis.

rite of reversal   A situation in which behaviour outside the social norms is acceptable to society.

satanic ritual abuse   Claims of child abuse associated with the rituals of satanists.

scientist-practitioner model   The scientific approach to treatment, involving hypothesis-testing and monitoring of response to treatment, as well as forging clear links between research and practice.

seduction theory   An early theory of Freud's that his patients' problems were the result of childhood seduction.

self-actualisation   The need of all individuals to realise their full potential.

self-monitoring   Asking clients to observe and record their own thoughts and behaviours.

social constructionism   The idea that our view of the world is constructed through social agreement and may therefore be open to change with time or culture.

social drift hypothesis   The suggestion that people with mental disorders may be downwardly mobile.

social learning   Bandura's theory that behaviour can be learned from other people through the processes of observation, imitation and reinforcement.

social norms   Expectations of behaviour that are enforced by a particular society.

sociogenic hypothesis   The proposal that social conditions may be responsible for the observed class differences in the rates of mental disorder.

split-half reliability   A method of estimating the reliability of a test by comparing scores on half of the test items with scores on the other half (where items can be randomly divided into two groups).

state-dependent learning The theory that information learned when the individual is in a particular state will be best recalled when the individual is in the same state.

subculture A subdivision within a cultural group, which shares distinctive behaviours, beliefs and attitudes.

suppression–facilitation model The idea that a culture may suppress or facilitate particular behaviours, leading to differences in what is considered abnormal.

symbolic healing The use of culturally accepted symbols and rituals to promote recovery.

test–retest reliability The degree of consistency in test results over time.

transcultural psychiatry/psychology An integrated attempt to account for cultural differences in behaviour.

trauma-dissociation model An explanation for MPD that suggests early trauma has been dealt with by dissociation to create sub-personalities, some of whom have no memory of the trauma.

universality The view that the same mental disorders occur in all cultures.

validity The extent to which a test, an experiment or a diagnosis really represents what it claims to represent.

Bibliography

Acharyya, S. (1996). Practising cultural psychiatry: The doctor's dilemma. In T. Heller, J. Reynolds, R. Gomm, P. Muston & S. Pattison (eds) *Mental Health Matters*. Basingstoke, UK: Macmillan.

Acocella, J. (1999). *Creating Hysteria: Women and Multiple Personality Disorder*. San Francisco: Jossey Bass.

Adityanjee, R. & Khandelwal, S. (1989). Current status of multiple personality disorder in India. *American Journal of Psychiatry*, *146*, 1607–1610.

Adler, D., Drake, R., & Teague, G. (1990). Clinicians' practices in personality assessment. *Comprehensive Psychiatry*, *31*, 125–133.

Aldridge-Morris, R. (1989). *Multiple Personality: An Exercise in Deception*. Hove, UK: Lawrence Erlbaum Associates Ltd.

Allen, J. (1993) Dissociative processes: Theoretical underpinnings of a working model for clinician and patient. *Bulletin of Menninger Clinic*, *57*(3), 287–308.

Allison, R. (1978). On discovering multiplicity. *Sven Tidskr Hypnos*, *2*, 4–8.

American Psychological Association (1994) *Diagnostic and Statistical Manual of Mental Disorders* (4th edition). Washington: APA.

Andreasen, N., Swayze, V., Tyrrell, G., Arndt, S. & McChesney, C. (1990). Ventricular enlargement in schizophrenia evaluated with computed tomographic scanning. *Archives of General Psychiatry*, *47*, 1008–1015.

Antonovsky, A. (1979). *Health, Stress and Coping*. San Francisco: Jossey Bass.

Apter, A. (1991). The problem of Who: Multiple personality, personal identity, and the double brain. *Philosophical Psychology*, *4*(2), 219–248.

Arrigo, J. & Pezdek, K. (1998). Textbook models of multiple personality. In S. Lynn & K. McConkey (eds) *Truth in Memory*. NY: Guilford Press.

Bandura, A (1969). *Principles of Behaviour Modification*. NY: Rinehart & Winston.

Banister, P. et al. (1994). *Qualitative Methods in Psychology: A Research Guide*. Buckingham, UK: Open University Press.

Banyard, P. (1996). *Applying Psychology to Health*. London: Hodder & Stoughton.

Barkley, R. (1981). *Hyperactive Children: A Handbook for Diagnosis and Treatment*. NY: Guilford Press.

Barlow, D. (1977). Behavioural assessment in clinical settings. In J. Cone & R. Hawkins (eds) *Behavioural Assessment: New Directions in Clinical Psychology*. NY: Brunner Mazel.

Barraclough, B. (1988). International variation in the suicide rate of 15–24 year-olds. *Social Psychiatry and Psychiatric Epidemiology*, *23*(2), 75–84.

Bass, E. & Davis, L. (1988). *The Courage to Heal*. NY: Harper & Row.

Bateson, G., Jackson, D., Haley, J. & Weakland, J. (1956). Towards a theory of schizophrenia. *Behavioural Science*, *1*, 251–264.

Baxter, L. et al. (1987). Local cerebral glucose metabolic rates in obsessive compulsive disorder. *Archives of General Psychiatry*, *44*, 211–218.

Bean, P. & Mounser, P. (1993). *Discharge from Mental Hospitals*. London: Macmillan.

Bebbington, P. et al. (1989). The risk of minor depression before the age of 65: Results from a community survey. *Psychological Medicine*, *19*(2), 393–400.

Beck, A. (1963). Thinking and depression. *Archives of General Psychiatry*, *9*, 324–333.

Beck, A. et al. (1962). Reliability of psychiatric diagnoses. *American Journal of Psychiatry*, *119*, 351–357.

Beck, A., Steer, R. & Garbin, M. (1988). Psychometric properties of the Beck Depression Inventory: Twenty-five years of evaluation. *Clinical Psychology Review*, *8*, 77–100.

Becker, D. & Lamb, S. (1994). Sex bias in the diagnosis of borderline personality disorder and post-traumatic stress disorder. *Professional Psychology, Research and Practice*, *25*, 55–61.

Becker, H. (1963). *Outsiders: Studies in the Sociology of Deviance*. NY: Free Press.

Bell, C. (2000). *Counteracting Traumatic Stress in Black Children*. Paper given to 'Visibility and invisibility' conference, Leeds Community and Mental Health Services Trust, 13–14 April.

Bender, L. (1938). *A Visual Motor Gestalt test and its Clinical Use*. NY: American Orthopsychiatric Association.

Bentovim, A. & Tranter, M. (1994). Psychotherapeutic work with adult survivors of child sexual abuse. In P. Clarkson & M. Pokorny (eds) *The Handbook of Psychotherapy*. London: Routledge.

Bernstein, E. & Putnam, W. (1986). Development, reliability and validity of a dissociation scale. *Journal of Nervous and Mental Diseases*, *174*(12), 727–735.

Berrios, G. and Morley, S. (1984). Koro-like symptoms in a non-Chinese subject. *British Journal of Psychiatry*, *145*, 331–4.

Berry, J. et al. (1992). *Cross-cultural Psychology*. Cambridge: Cambridge University Press.

Binitie, A. (1970). Attitude of educated Nigerians to psychiatric illness. *Acta Psychiatrica Scandinavica*, *46*, 29–34.

Blake, W. (1973). The influence of race on diagnosis. *Smith College Studies in Social Work*, *43*(3), 184–192.

Blashfield, R. & Draguns, J. (1976). Evaluative criteria for psychiatric classification. *Journal of Abnormal Psychology*, *85*, 140–150.

Blaxter, M. (1990). *Health and Lifestyles*. London: Routledge.

Bliss, E. (1980). Multiple personalities: A report of 14 cases with implications for schizophrenia and hysteria. *Archives of General Psychiatry*, *37*, 1388–1397.

Bliss, E. (1986). *Multiple Personality, Allied Disorders and Hypnosis*. NY: Oxford University Press.

Boddy, J. (1989). *Wombs and Alien Spirits: Women, Men and the Zar Cult in Northern Sudan*. Madison, WI: University of Wisconsin Press.

Bolton, P. (1984). Management of compulsorily admitted patients to a high security unit. *International Journal of Social Psychiatry*, *30*, 77–84.

Bolton, R. (1981). Susto, hostility and hypoglycaemia. *Ethnology*, *20*, 261–276.

Boon, S. & Draijer, N. (1993). Multiple personality disorder in the Netherlands: A clinical investigation of 71 patients. *American Journal of Psychiatry*, *150*, 489–494.

Boskind-Lodahl, M. & White W. (1978). The definition and treatment of bulimarexia in college women – a pilot study. *Journal of American College Health Association*, *27*, 84–97.

Bourguignon, E. (1973). Introduction: A framework for the comparative study of altered states of consciousness. In E. Bourguignon (ed) *Religion, Altered States of Consciousness and Social Change*. Columbus: Ohio State University Press.

Braun, B. (1990). Multiple personality disorder: An overview. *American Journal of Occupational Therapy*, *44*(11), 971–976.

British Psychological Society (2000). Guidelines for psychologists working with clients in contexts in which issues related to recovered memories may arise. *The Psychologist*, *13*(5), 266.

Broverman, I. et al. (1981). Sex role stereotypes and clinical judgements of mental health. In E. Howell & M. Bayes (eds) *Women and Mental Health*. NY: Basic Books.

Brown, G. (1996). Onset and course of depressive disorders: A summary of a research programme. In C. Mundt et al. (eds) *Interpersonal Factors in the Origin and Course of Affective Disorders*. London: Gaskell.

Brown, G. & Harris, T. (1978). *Social Origins of Depression: A Study of Psychiatric Disorder in Women*. NY: Free Press.

Brown, G., Harris, T. & Hepworth, C. (1995). Loss, humiliation and entrapment among women developing depression. *Psychological Medicine*, *25*(1), 7–21.

Brown, G., Monck, E., Carstairs, G. & Wing, J. (1962). Influence of family life on the course of schizophrenic illness. *British Journal of Preventative and Social Medicine*, *3*, 74–87.

Bruce, M., Takeuchi, D. & Leaf, P. (1991). Poverty and psychiatric status: Longitudinal evidence from the New Haven Epidemiological Catchment Area Study. *Archives of General Psychiatry*, 48, 470–474.

Burke, K., Burke, J., Regier, D. & Rae, D. (1990). Age at onset of selected mental disorders in five community populations. *Archives of General Psychiatry*, *47*, 511–518.

Busfield, J. (1996). *Men, Women and Madness*. Basingstoke, UK: Macmillan.

Canino, G. et al. (1987). The prevalence of specific psychiatric disorders in Puerto Rico. *Archives of General Psychiatry, 44*, 727–735.

Cardena, E. & Spiegel, D. (1993). Dissociative reactions to the San Francisco Bay area earthquake of 1989. *American Journal of Psychiatry, 150*, 474–478.

Carlson, E. & Putnam, F. (1993). An update on the Dissociative Experiences Scale. *Dissociation, 6*, 16–27.

Carlson, E., Putnam, F. et al. (1993). Validity of the Dissociative Experiences Scale in screening for multiple personality. *American Journal of Psychiatry, 150*, 1030–1036.

Carlson, G. & Cantwell, D. (1980). Unmasking masked depression in children and adolescents. *American Journal of Psychiatry, 137*, 445–449.

Carpenter, I. & Brockington, I. (1980). A study of mental illness in Asians, West Indians and Africans living in Manchester. *British Journal of Psychiatry, 137*, 201–205.

Carr, A. (1999). *Handbook of Child and Adolescent Clinical Psychology*. London: Routledge.

Carr, J. (1985). Ethno-behaviourism and the culture-bound syndromes: The case of amok. In R. Simons & C. Hughes (eds) *The Culture-bound Syndromes: Folk Illnesses of Psychiatric and Anthropological Interest*. Dordrecht: D. Reidl.

Carstairs, G. & Kapur, R. (1976). *The Great Universe of Kota: Stress, Change and Mental Disorder in an Indian Village*. Berkeley: University of California Press.

Castillo, R. (1991). *Culture, Trance and Mental Illness: Divided Consciousness in South Asia*. Unpublished doctoral dissertation, Harvard University, Cambridge, MA.

Castillo, R. (1995). Culture, trance and the mind-brain. *Anthropology of Consciousness, 6*, 17–34.

Castillo, R. (1997). *Culture and Mental Illness*. Pacific Grove, CA: Brooks-Cole.

Catalano, R., Hawkins, J., Krenz, C., Gillmore, M., Morrison, D., Wells, E. & Abbott, R. (1993). Using research to guide culturally appropriate drug abuse prevention. *Journal of Consulting and Clinical Psychology, 61*, 804–811.

Chesler, P. (1972). *Women and Madness*. NY: Doubleday.

Clipson, C. & Steer, J. (1998). *Case Studies in Abnormal Psychology*. Boston: Houghton Mifflin.

Cochrane, R. (1977). Mental illness in immigrants to England and Wales. *Social Psychiatry, 12*, 25–35.

Cochrane, R. (1995). Women and depression. *Psychology Review, 2*, 20–24.

Cochrane, R. & Bal, S. (1989). Mental hospital admission rates of immigrants to England: A comparison of 1971 and 1981. *Social Psychiatry, 24*, 2–11.

Cochrane, R. & Sashidharan, S. (1995). *Mental Health and Ethnic Minorities: A Review of the Literature and Implications for Services*. Paper presented to the Birmingham and North Birmingham Health Trust.

Cochrane, R. & Stopes-Roe, M. (1981). Women, marriage, employment and mental health. *British Journal of Psychiatry, 139*, 373–381.

Collomb, H. (1966). Bouffées délirantes en psychiatrie Africaine. *Transcultural Psychiatric Research, 3*, 29–34.

Colson, A. (1971). The perception of abnormality in a Malay village. In N. Wagner & E. Tan (eds) *Psychological Problems and Treatment in Malaysia*. Kuala Lumpur: University of Malaya Press.

Comer, R. (1998). *Abnormal Psychology*. NY: W.H. Freeman.

Compton, W. et al. (1991). New methods in cross-cultural psychiatry. *American Journal of Psychiatry, 148*(12), 1697–1704.

Connors, C.A. (1969). Teacher rating scale for use in drug studies with children. *American Journal of Psychiatry, 126*, 884–888.

Coons, P. (1986). The prevalence of multiple personality disorder. *Newsletter, International Society for the Study of Multiple Personality and Dissociation, 4*(3), 6–8.

Coons, P. (1991). Iatrogenesis and malingering of multiple personality disorder in the forensic evaluation of homicide defendants. *Psychiatric Clinics of North America, 14*(3), 757–768.

Coons, P. (1994). Confirmation of child abuse in child and adolescent cases of multiple personality disorder and dissociative disorder not otherwise specified. *Journal of Nervous and Mental Disease, 182*, 461–464.

Coons, P. & Milstein, V. (1994). Factitious or malingered multiple personality disorder: Eleven cases. *Dissociation, 7*(2), 81–85.

Cooper, M., Russell, M. & George, W. (1988). Coping, expectations and alcohol abuse: A test of social learning formulations. *Journal of Abnormal Psychology*, *97*, 218–230.

Copeland, J. et al. (1971). Differences in the usage of psychiatric labels amongst psychiatrists in the British Isles. *British Journal of Psychiatry*, *118*(547), 629–640.

Copeland, J. et al. (1987). Range of mental illness among the elderly in the community. *British Journal of Psychiatry*, *150*, 815–823.

Corby, B. (2000). *Child Abuse: Towards a Knowledge Base*. Buckingham, UK: Open University Press.

Costello, E., Edelbrock, C. & Costello, A. (1985). The validity of the NIMH Diagnostic Interview Schedule for Children. *Journal of Abnormal Child Psychology*, *13*(4), 579–595.

Costello, T., Costello, J. & Holmes, D. (1995). *Abnormal Psychology*. London: HarperCollins.

Cross-national Collaborative Group (1992). The changing rate of major depression: Cross-national comparisons. *Journal of the American Medical Association*, *268*, 3098–3105.

Daly, M. & Wilson, M. (1994). Some differential attributes of lethal assaults on small children by stepfathers versus genetic fathers. *Ethology and Sociobiology*, *15*, 207–217.

Davey, G. et al. (1998). A cross-cultural study of animal fears. *Behaviour Research and Therapy*, *36*(7–8), 735–750.

Davies, J. & Frawley, M. (1991). Dissociative processes and transference–countertransference paradigms in the psychoanalytically oriented treatment of adult survivors of child sexual abuse. *Psychoanalytic Dialogues*, *2*, 5–36.

Davison, G. & Neale, J. (1994). *Abnormal Psychology*. NY: Wiley.

Dawson, J. (1999). The alter as agent: Multiple personality and the insanity defence. *Psychiatry, Psychology and Law*, *6*(2) 203–206.

Dennis, P. (1985). Grisi siknis in Miskito culture. In R. Simons & C. Hughes (eds) *The Culture-bound Syndromes: Folk Illnesses of Psychiatric and Anthropological Interest*. Dordrecht: D. Reidel.

Derogatis, L. (1977). *SCL-R-90: Administration, Scoring and Procedures Manual*. Baltimore: Clinical Psychometrics Research.

Dick, L. (1995). 'Pibloktoq' (Arctic hysteria): A construction of European–Inuit relation? *Arctic Anthropology*, *32*(2), 1–42.

Di Nardo, P. et al. (1993). Reliability of DSM III-R anxiety disorder categories. *Archives of General Psychiatry*, *50*, 251–256.

Dohrenwend, B., Levav, I., Shrou, P., Schwartz, S., Naveh, G., Link, B., Skodol, A. & Stueve, A. (1992). Socio-economic status and psychiatric disorders: The causation–selection issue. *Science, 255,* 946–952.

Dover, S. & McWilliam, C. (1992). Physical illness associated with depression in the elderly in community based and hospital patients. *Psychiatric Bulletin, 16,* 612–3.

Dow, J. (1986). Universal aspects of symbolic healing: A theoretical synthesis. *American Anthropologist, 88,* 56–69.

Dunham, H. (1965). *Community and Schizophrenia: An Epidemiological Analysis.* Detroit: Wayne State University Press.

Edgerton, R. (1971). *The Individual in Cultural Adaptation.* Berkeley: University of California Press.

Eich, E. (1995). Searching for mood-dependent memory. *Psychological Science, 6*(2), 67–75.

Erdberg, P. & Exner, J. (1984). Personality assessment: Rorschach assessment. In G. Goldstein & M. Hersen (eds) *Handbook of Psychological Assessment.* NY: Pergamon Press.

Erikson, K. (1976). *Everything in its Path: Destruction of a Community in the Buffalo Creek Flood.* NY: Simon & Schuster.

Erinosho, O. & Ayonrinde, A. (1981). Educational background and attitudes to mental illness among the yoruba in Nigeria. *Human Relations, 34,* 1–12.

Falek, A. & Moser, H. (1975). Classification in schizophrenia. *Archives of General Psychiatry, 32,* 59–67.

Faris, R. & Dunham, H. (1939). *Mental Disorders in Urban Areas.* Chicago: University of Chicago Press.

Fernando, S. (1988). *Race and Culture in Psychiatry.* London: Croom Helm.

Fernando, S. (1991). *Mental Health, Race and Culture.* London: Macmillan/MIND.

Fernando, S. (ed.) (1995) *Mental Health in a Multi-ethnic Society.* London: Routledge.

Fewtrell, W. (1981). *Variations in Clinical Opinion Between Psychologists Treating a Single Case of Sleep Dysfunction.* Annual conference, British Psychological Society.

Finkler, K. (1981). Non-medical treatments and their outcomes. Part two: Focus on the adherents of spiritualism. *Culture, Medicine and Psychiatry, 5,* 65–103.

Fitzpatrick, K. and Boldizar, J. (1993) The prevalence and consequences of exposure to violence among African's American youth. *Journal of the American Academy of Child and Adolescent Psychiatry, 32*(2), 424–430.

Flaskerud, J. (2000). Ethnicity, culture and neuropsychiatry. *Issues in Mental Health Nursing, 21*, 5–29.

Ford, M. & Widiger, T. (1989). Sex bias in the diagnosis of histrionic and antisocial personality disorders. *Journal of Consulting and Clinical Psychology, 57*, 301–305.

Foster, G. & Anderson, B. (1978). *Medical Anthropology.* NY: Wiley.

Frederick, J. (1991). *Positive Thinking for Mental Health.* London: The Black Mental Health Group.

French, A. & Schechmeister, J. (1983). The multiple personality syndrome and criminal defence. *Bulletin of the American Academy of Psychiatry and the Law, 11*(1), 17–25.

Frick, W. (1995). The subpersonalities controversy. *Journal of Human Psychology, 35*(1), 97–101.

Fryer, D. (1995). Labour market disadvantage, deprivation and mental health. *The Psychologist, 8*(6), 265–272.

Furnham, A. & Malik, R. (1994). Cross-cultural beliefs about depression. *International Journal of Social Psychiatry, 40*, 106–123.

Ganaway, G. (1989). Historical versus narrative truth: Clarifying the role of exogenous trauma in the etiology of MPD and its variants. *Dissociation, 2*(4) 205–220.

Garb, H. (1997). Race bias, social class bias and gender bias in clinical judgement. *Clinical Psychology: Science and Practice, 4*, 99–120.

Gardner, H. (1983). *Frames of Mind: The Theory of Multiple Intelligences.* NY: Basic Books.

Gelfand, M. (1964). Psychiatric disorders as recognised by the Shona. In A. Kiev (ed), *Magic, Faith and Healing.* NY: Free Press.

Gilbertson, A. et al. (1992). Susceptibility of common self-report measures of dissociation to malingering. *Dissociation, 5*, 216–220.

Goff, D. & Sims, C. (1993). Has multiple personality disorder remained constant over time? *Journal of Nervous and Mental Disease, 181*, 595–600.

Goffman, E. (1968). *Asylums.* Harmondsworth, UK: Penguin.

Gold, E. (1986). Long-term effects of sexual victimization in childhood. *Journal of Consulting and Clinical Psychology, 54*, 471–475.

Goldberg, D. & Williams, P. (1988). *A User's Guide to the General Health Questionnaire*. Windsor, UK: NFER Nelson.

Goldberg, E. & Morrison, S. (1963). Schizophrenia and social class. *British Journal of Psychiatry, 109*, 785–802.

Goodwin, C. (1995). *Research in Psychology*. NY: Wiley.

Greaves, G. (1980). Multiple Personality: 165 years after Mary Reynolds. *Journal of Nervous and Mental Diseases, 168*, 577–596.

Gross. R. (1992). *Psychology: The Science of Mind and Behaviour*. London: Hodder & Stoughton.

Gross, R. (1994) *Key Studies in Psychology*. London: Hodder & Stoughton.

Gross, R. & McIlveen, R. (1998). *Psychology: A New Introduction*. London: Hodder & Stoughton.

Guarnaccia, P. (1993). Ataques de nervios in Puerto Rico: Culture-bound syndrome or popular illness? *Medical Anthropology, 15*, 157–170.

Guarnaccia, P., De La Cancela, V. & Carrillo, E. (1989). The multiple meanings of ataques de nervios in the Latino community. *Medical Anthropology, 11*, 47–62.

Guarnaccia, P., Good, B. & Kleinman, A. (1990). A critical review of epidemiological studies of Puerto Rican Mental Health. *American Journal of Psychiatry, 147*, 1449–1455.

Guarnaccia, P., Rivera, M. et al. (1996). The experiences of ataques de nervios: Towards an anthropology of emotions in Puerto Rico. *Culture, Medicine and Psychiatry, 20*, 343–367.

Hacking, I. (1995). *Rewriting the Soul: Multiple Personality and the Sciences of Memory*. NJ: Princeton.

Halgin, R.P. & Whitbourne, S.K. (1993). *Abnormal Psychology: The Human Experience of Psychological Disorders*. NY: Harcourt Brace.

Halpern, D. (1995). *Mental Health and the Built Environment*. London: Taylor & Francis.

Harrison, G. et al. (1988). A prospective study of severe mental disorder in Afro-Caribbean patients. *Psychological Medicine, 18*, 643–657.

Harrison, P. et al. (1998). *Lecture Notes on Psychiatry*. Oxford: Blackwell.

Hartocollis, L. (1998). The making of multiple personality disorder. *Clinical Social Work Journal, 26*(2) 159–176.

Hathaway, S. & McKinley, J. (1943). *Manual for the Minnesota Multiphasic Personality Inventory*. NY: Psychological Corporation.

Heather, N. (1976). *Radical Perspectives in Psychology*. London: Methuen.

Helman, C. (1984). *Culture, Health and Illness*. London: Wright PSG.

Helzer, J., Canino, G., Yeh, E., Bland, R., Lee, C., Hwu, H., & Newman, S. (1990). Alcoholism: North America and Asia – a comparison of population surveys with the Diagnostic Interview Schedule. *Archives of General Psychiatry*, *47*, 313–319.

Heyman, I and Fahy, T. (1992). Koro-like symptoms in a man infected with the human immunodeficiency virus. *British Journal of Psychiatry*, *160*, 119–121.

Hilgard, E. (1977). *Divided Consciousness: Multiple Controls on Human Thought and Action*. NY: Wiley.

Hitch, P. (1981). Immigration and mental health: Local research and social explanations. *New Community*, *9*, 256–262.

Hollingshead, A. & Redlich, F. (1958). *Social Class and Mental Illness*. NY: Wiley.

Holmes, D. (1994). *Abnormal Psychology*. NY: HarperCollins.

Hornstein, N. & Putnam, F. (1992). Clinical phenomenology of child and adolescent dissociative disorders. *American Academy of Child and Adolescent Psychiatry*, *31*, 1077–1085.

Hornstein, N. & Tyson, S. (1991). Inpatient treatment of children with multiple personality/dissociative disorders and their families. *Psychiatric Clinics of North America*, *14*, 631–638.

Hussain, M. & Gomersall, J. (1978). Affective disorder in Asian immigrants. *Psychiatrica Clinica*, *11*, 87–89.

Jablensky, A. et al. (1992). Schizophrenia: Manifestations, course and incidence in different cultures. *Psychological Medicine Monograph Supplement 20*.

Jahoda, M. (1958). *Current Concepts of Positive Mental Health*. NY: Basic Books.

James, D. & Schramm, M. (1998). Multiple personality disorder presenting to the English courts: A case study. *Journal of Forensic Psychiatry*, *9*(3) 618–628.

Jampala, V., Sierles, F. & Taylor, M. (1986). Consumers' views of DSM III: Attitudes and practices of U.S. psychiatrists and 1984 graduate residents. *American Journal of Psychiatry*, *143*, 148–153.

Johnstone, L. (1989). *Users and Abusers of Psychiatry*. London: Routledge.

Johnstone, T. (1987). Premenstrual syndrome as a Western culture-specific disorder. *Culture, Medicine and Psychiatry, 11*, 337–356.

Karno, M., Hough, R., Burnam, M., Escobar, J., Yimbers, D., Santana, F. & Boyd, J. (1987). Lifetime prevalence of specific psychiatric disorders among Mexican Americans and non-Hispanic whites in Los Angeles. *Archives of General Psychiatry, 44*, 695–701.

Kelly, K. (1993). Multiple personality disorders: Treatment co-ordination in a partial hospital setting. *Bulletin of Menninger Clinic, 57*(3), 390–398.

Kempe, C. et al. (1962). The battered child syndrome. *Journal of the American Medical Association, 181*(1), 17–24.

Kendall, P. & Hammen, C. (1995). *Abnormal Psychology*. Boston: Houghton Mifflin.

Kendall, P. & Norton-Ford, J. (1982). *Clinical Psychology*. London: Wiley.

Kendall-Tackett, K., Williams, L. & Finkelhor, D. (1993). Impact of sexual abuse on children: A review. *Psychological Bulletin, 113*, 164–180.

Kendell, R. (1975). *The Role of Diagnosis in Psychiatry*. Oxford: Blackwell.

Kenny, M. (1986). *The passion of Ansel Bourne*. Washington, DC: Smithsonian.

Kessler, R. et al. (1994). Lifetime and 12-month prevalence of DSM III-R psychiatric disorders in the United States. *Archives of General Psychiatry, 51*, 8–19.

Kety, S. (1974). From rationalisation to reason. *American Journal of Psychiatry, 131*, 957–962.

Keyes, D. (1981). *The Minds of Billy Milligan*. NY: Random House.

Khandelwal, S., Sharan, P. & Saxena, S. (1995). Eating disorders: An Indian perspective. *International Journal of Social Psychiatry, 41*, 132–146.

Kiev, A. (1972). *Transcultural Psychiatry*. NY: Free Press.

Kihlstrom, J. (1995). Dissociative disorders. In H. Adams & P. Suther (eds) *Comprehensive Handbook of Psychopathology*. NY: Plenum Press.

Kim, K. et al. (1993). Schizophrenic delusions among Koreans, Korean-Chinese and Chinese: A transcultural study. *International Journal of Social Psychiatry, 39*, 190–199.

Kirmayer, L. et al. (1996). *Pathways and Barriers to Mental Health*

Care: A Community Survey and Ethnographic Study. Montreal: Sir Mortimer B. Davis Jewish General Hospital.

Kirmayer, L. & Minas, H. (2000). The future of cultural psychiatry: An international perspective. *Canadian Journal of Psychiatry*, *45*, 438–446.

Klein, P. et al. (1993). *DSM IV: 1993 Update.* NY: W.H. Freeman.

Kleinman, A. (1980). *Patients and Healers in the Context of Culture.* Berkeley: University of California Press.

Kleinman, A. (1991). *Culture and DSM IV: Recommendations for the Introduction and for the Overall Structure.* Paper presented to the NIHM conference on Culture and Diagnosis, Pittsburgh, April.

Kleinman, A. & Cohen, A. (1997). Psychiatry's global challenge. *Scientific American, March*, 86–89.

Kline, M. (1952). A note on 'primate-like' behaviour induced through hypnosis: A case report. *Journal of General Psychology*, *81*, 125–131.

Kline, P. (1993). *The Handbook of Psychological Testing.* NY: Routledge.

Kluft, R. (1987). The simulation and dissimulation of multiple personality disorder. *American Journal of Clinical Hypnosis*, *30*(2) 104–118.

Kluft, R. (1995). The confirmation or disconfirmation of memories of abuse in DID patients: A naturalistic clinical study. *Dissociation*, *8*(4) 253–258.

Kluft, R. (1998). Reflections on the traumatic memories of dissociative identity disorder patients. In S. Lynn & K. McConkey (eds) *Truth in Memory*. NY: Guilford Press.

Knutson, J. (1995). Psychological characteristics of maltreated children. In J. Spence et al. (eds) *Annual Review of Psychology*, *46*, 401–431.

Kraepelin, E. (1883). *Lehrbuch der Psychiatrie* [translated by A. Diefendorf]. Delmar, NY: Scholars' Facsimiles and Reprints.

Landrine, H. (1991). Revising the framework of abnormal psychology. In P. Bronstein & K. Quina (eds) *Teaching a Psychology of People*. Washington, DC: APA.

Langer, E. & Abelson, R. (1974). A patient by any other name: Clinician group difference in labelling bias. *Journal of Consulting and Clinical Psychology*, *42*, 4–9.

Langwieler, G. & Linden, M. (1993). Therapist individuality in the diagnosis and treatment of depression. *Journal of Affective Disorders*, *27*, 1–12.

Lau, B., Kung, N. & Chung, J. (1983). How depressive illness presents in Hong Kong. *Practitioner*, *227*, 112–114.

Laurence, J., Day, D. & Gaston, L. (1998). From memories of abuse to the abuse of memories. In S. Lynn & K. McConkey (eds) *Truth in Memory*. NY: Guilford Press.

Lavender, T. (2000). Schizophrenia. In L. Champion & M. Power (eds), *Adult Psychological Problems*. Hove, UK: Psychology Press.

Lee, S. (1993). Side effects of lithium therapy in Hong Kong Chinese. *Culture, Medicine and Psychiatry*, *17*(3), 301–320.

Lee, S., Ho, T. & Hsu, L. (1993). Fat phobic and non-fat phobic anorexia nervosa: A comparative study of 70 Chinese patients in Hong Kong. *Psychological Medicine*, *23*, 999–1017.

Lee, S. & Hsu, G. (1995). Eating disorders in Hong Kong. In T. Lin, W. Tseng & E. Yeh (eds) *Chinese societies and Mental Health*. NY: Oxford University Press.

Leng, G. (1985). Koro: A cultural disease. In R. Simons & C. Hughes (eds) *The Culture-bound Syndromes: Folk Illnesses of Psychiatric and Anthropological Interest*. Boston: D. Reidel.

Lewis, D. & Bard, J. (1991). Multiple personality and forensic issues. *Psychiatric Clinics of North America*, *14*(3), 741–756.

Lewis, D. et al. (1997). Objective documentation of child abuse and dissociation in 12 murderers with dissociative identity disorder. *American Journal of Psychiatry*, *154*, 1703–1710.

Lewis-Fernandez, R. (1997). A cultural critique of the DSM IV Dissociative Disorders section. *Transcultural Psychiatry*, *35*(3), 387–400.

Lin, K. (1996). Psychopharmacology in cross-cultural psychiatry. *Mount Sinai Journal of Medicine*, *63*, 283–284.

Lindsay, S. & Powell, G. (eds) (1994). *The Handbook of Clinical Adult Psychology*. London: Routledge.

Lipton, A. & Simon, F. (1985). Psychiatric diagnosis in a state hospital. *Hospital and Community Psychiatry*, *36*(4), 368–373.

Littlewood, R. (1992). Psychiatric diagnosis and racial bias. *Social Science and Medicine*, *34*, 141–149.

Littlewood, R. & Cross, S. (1980). Ethnic minorities and psychiatric services. *Sociology of Health and Illness*, *2*, 194–201.

Littlewood, R. & Lipsedge, M. (1989) *Aliens and Alienists: Ethnic Minorities and Psychiatry*. London: Unwin Hyman.

Loftus, E. (1993). The reality of repressed memories. *American Psychologist*, *48*, 518–537.

London et al. (1969). [Cited in Gross. R. (1994). *Key Studies in Psychology*, p. 347. London: Hodder & Stoughton.]

Lopez, S., Grover, K., Holland, D., Johnson, M., Kain, C., Kanel, K., Mellins, C. & Rhyne, M. (1989). Development of culturally sensitive psychotherapists. *Professional Psychology: Research and Practice*, *20*, 369–376.

Lopez, S. & Hernandez, P. (1986). How culture is considered in evaluations of psychopathology. *Journal of Nervous and Mental Disease*, *176*, 598–606.

Loring, M. & Powell, B. (1988). Gender, race and DSM-III: A study of the objectivity of psychiatric diagnostic behaviour. *Journal of Health and Social Behaviour*, *29*, 1–22.

Lowenthal, M. et al. (1965). *Ageing and Mental Disorder in San Francisco*. San Francisco: Jossey Bass.

Luchins, A. (1957). Primacy–recency in impression formation. In C. Hovland (ed) *The Order of Presentation in Persuasion*. Connecticut: Yale University Press.

Lutz, C. (1985). Depression and translation of emotional worlds. In A. Kleinman & B. Good (eds) *Culture and Depression: Studies in the Anthropology and Cross-cultural Psychiatry of Affect and Disorder*. Berkeley: University of California Press.

Maher, W. & Maher, B. (1985). Psychopathology: I From ancient times to the eighteenth century. In G. Kimble & K. Schlesinger (eds) *Topics in the History of Psychology*. Hillsdale, NJ: Lawrence Erlbaum Associates Inc.

Mair, K. (1997). *Psychological Treatment for Dissociative Identity Disorder: Risks and Benefits*. Paper given at BPS conference, London, 17 December.

Mair, K. (1999). Multiple personality and child abuse. *The Psychologist*, *12*(2), 76–80.

Mann, A., Graham, N. & Ashby, D. (1984). Psychiatric illness in residential homes for the elderly: A survey in one London borough. *Age and Ageing*, *113*, 257–65.

Marano, L. (1982). Windigo psychosis: The anatomy of an emic/etic confusion. *Current Anthropology*, *23*, 385–412.

Martinez-Taboas, M. (1991). Multiple personality disorder as seen from a social constructionist standpoint. *Dissociation, 4,* 189–192.

Masson, J. (1988). *Against Therapy.* London: Collins.

McCajor-Hall, T. (1998). *Glossary of Culture-bound Syndromes.* http://weber.ucsd.edu~thall/cbs_glos.html.

McCoy, S. (1976). Clinical judgements of normal childhood behaviour. *Journal of Consulting and Clinical Psychology, 44*(5), 710–714.

McDougall, W. (1938) *Body and Mind.* NY: Macmillan.

McGovern, D. & Cope, R. (1987). The compulsory detention of males of different ethnic groups with special reference to offender patients. *British Journal of Psychiatry, 150,* 505–512.

Meehl, P. (1960). The cognitive activity of the clinician. *American Psychology, 15,* 19–27.

Meehl, P. & Rosen, A. (1955). Antecedent probability and the efficiency of psychometric signs, patterns, or cutting scores. *Psychological Bulletin, 52,* 194–216.

Meltzer, H. et al. (1995). *OPCS Surveys of Psychiatric Morbidity in Great Britain: Report No. 1: The Prevalence of Psychiatric Morbidity among Adults Living in Private Households.* London: HMSO.

Mersky, H. (1992). The manufacture of personalities: The production of multiple personality disorder. *British Journal of Psychiatry, 160,* 327–340.

Mersky, H. (1995). Multiple personality disorder and false memory syndrome. *British Journal of Psychiatry, 166*(3), 281–283.

Mezzich, J. et al. (1989) DSM disorders in a large sample of psychiatric patients. *American Journal of Psychiatry, 146*(2), 212–219.

Mezzich, J., Kirmayer, L., Kleinman, A. et al. (1999). The place of culture in DSM IV. *Journal of Nervous and Mental Diseases, 187*(8), 457–464.

Miller, K. (1987). *Doubles: Studies in Literary History.* Oxford: Oxford University Press.

Minuchin, S., Rosman, B. & Baker, L. (1978). *Psychosomatic Families: Anorexia Nervosa in Context.* Cambridge, MA: Harvard University Press.

Mischel, W. (1968). *Personality and Assessment.* NY: Wiley.

Mitchill, S. (1817). Double consciousness, or duality of person in the same individual. *The Medical Repository of Original Essays and*

Intelligence Relative to Physic, Surgery, Chemistry and Natural History, etc, 18.

Modestin J. (1992). Multiple personality disorder in Switzerland. *American Journal of Psychiatry, 149,* 88–92.

Mukherjee, S. et al. (1983). Misdiagnosis of schizophrenia in bipolar patients: A multi-ethnic comparison. *American Journal of Psychology, 140,* 1571–1574.

Murphy, J. (1964). Psychotherapeutic aspects of Shamanism on St Lawrence Island, Alaska. In A. Kiev (ed) *Magic, Faith and Healing.* NY: Free Press.

Murray. H. (1971). *Thematic Apperception Test.* Cambridge: Harvard University Press.

Myers, A. (1896). The life history of a case of double or multiple personality. *Journal of Mental Science, 31,* 596–605.

Nasser, M. (1986). Comparative study of the prevalence of abnormal eating attitudes among Arab female students of both London and Cairo universities. *Psychological Medicine, 16,* 621–625.

Nathan, P. & Langenbucher, J. (1999). Psychopathology: Description and classification. *Annual Review Psychology, 50,* 79–107.

Neisser, U. et al. (1996). Intelligence: Knowns and unknowns. *American Psychology, 51*(2) 77–101.

Nelson, R., Lipinski, D. & Black, J. (1975). The effects of expectancy on the reactivity of self-recording. *Behaviour Therapy, 6,* 337–349.

North, C., Ryall, J., Ricci, D. & Wetzel, R. (1993). *Multiple Personalities, Multiple Disorders: Psychiatric Classification and Media Influence.* Oxford: Oxford University Press.

Obeyesekere, G. (1977). The theory and practice of psychological medicine in the Ayurvedic tradition. *Culture, Medicine and Psychiatry, 1,* 155–181.

Okasha, A. et al. (1993). Diagnostic agreement in psychiatry: A comparative study between ICD-9, ICD-10 and DSM-III-R. *British Journal of Psychiatry, 162,* 621–626.

Orbach, S. (1978). *Fat is a Feminist Issue.* NY: Paddington.

Orne, M., Dunges, D. & Orne, E. (1984). On the differential diagnosis of multiple personality in the forensic context. *International Journal of Clinical and Experimental Hypnosis, 32,* 118–169.

Osgood, C., Suci, G. & Tannenbaum, P. (1957). *The Measurement of Meaning.* Urbana, IL: University of Illinois Press.

Ott, A., et al. (1995). Prevalence of Alzheimer's disease and vascular dementia-association with education – the Rotterdam study. *British Journal of Medical Psychology*, *310*(6985), 970–973.

Pang, K. (1990). Hwa-byung: The construction of a Korean popular illness among Korean elderly immigrant women in the United States. *Culture, Medicine and Psychiatry*, *14*, 495–512.

Parsons, T. (1951). *The Social System*. Glencoe, IL: Free Press.

Patterson, G., Chamberlain, P. & Reid, J. (1982). A comparative evaluation of a parent training program. *Behaviour Therapy*, *13*, 638–650.

Paul, G. (1966). *Insight vs. Desensitisation in Psychotherapy: An Experiment in Anxiety Reduction*. Stanford, CA: Stanford University Press.

Paurohit, N. et al. (1982). The role of verbal and nonverbal cues in the formation of first impressions of black and white counsellors. *Journal of Counselling Psychology*, *29*(4), 371–378.

Pearson, V. (1995). Goods on which one loses: Women and mental health in China. *Social Science and Medicine*, *41*(8), 1159–1173.

Perr, I. (1991). Crime and multiple personality. *Bulletin of the American Academy of Psychiatry and Law*, *19*, 203–214.

Peters, S. (1986). Child sexual abuse and later psychological problems. In M. Horowitz (ed) *Lasting Effects of Child Sexual Abuse*. Newbury Park, CA: Sage.

Phares, E. (1979). *Clinical Psychology: Concepts, Methods and Profession*. Homewood, IL: Dorsey.

Pilgrim, D. (2000). Psychiatric diagnosis: More questions than answers. *The Psychologist*, *13*(6) 302–305.

Pilgrim, D. & Rogers, A. (1999). *A Sociology of Mental Health and Illness*. Bucks, UK: Open University Press.

Pope, H., Oliva, P., Hudson, J., Bodkin, A. & Gruber, A. (1999). Attitudes toward DSM IV diagnoses among board-certified American psychiatrists. *American Journal of Psychiatry*, *156*(2), 321–323.

Power, M., Champion, L. & Aris, S. (1988). The development of a measure of social support: The Significant Others Scale. *British Journal of Clinical Psychology*, *27*, 349–358.

Prentice, P. (1996) Psychopathology. In M. Cardwell et al. (eds). *Psychology for A-level*. London: Collins Educational.

Prince, R. (1964). Indigenous Yoruba psychiatry. In A. Kiev (ed) *Magic, Faith and Healing*. NY: Free Press.

Prince, R. (1983). Is anorexia nervosa a culture-bound syndrome? *Transcultural Psychiatric Research Review, 20,* 299–300.

Putnam, F. (1984). The psychophysiologic investigation of multiple personality disorder. *Psychiatric Clinics of North America, 7,* 31–40.

Putnam, F. (1989). *Diagnosis and Treatment of Multiple Personality Disorder.* NY: Guilford Press.

Putnam, F. (1992). Dr Putnam's response. In J. Chu, The critical issues task force report. *ISSMP&D News, June,* 7–8.

Putnam, F. (1997). *Dissociation in Children and Adolescents.* NY: Guilford Press.

Putnam, F. Guroff, J., Silberman, E., Barban, L. & Post, R. (1986). The clinical phenomenology of multiple personality disorder: A review of 100 recent cases. *Journal of Clinical Psychiatry, 47*(6) 285–293.

Rack, P. (1982). *Culture and Mental Disorder.* London: Tavistock.

Reitan, R. & Davison, L. (1974). *Clinical neuropsychology: Current status and applications.* Washington, DC: V.H. Winston & Sons.

Rieber, R. (1999). Hypnosis, false memory and multiple personality: A trinity of affinity. *History of Psychiatry, 10,* 3–11.

Riley, K. (1988). Measurement of dissociation. *Journal of Nervous and Mental Disease, 176,* 149–150.

Ritenbaugh, C., Shisslak, C. & Prince, R. (1992). Eating disorders: A cross-cultural review in regard to DSM-IV. In J. Mezzich et al. (eds) *Cultural Proposals for DSM-IV. Submitted to the DSM-IV Task Force by The NIMH Group on Culture and Diagnosis.* Pittsburgh: University of Pittsburgh.

Robins, L., Helzer, J., Croughan, J. & Ratcliff, K. (1981). National Institute of Mental Health Diagnostic Interview Schedule: Its history, characteristics and validity. *Archives of General Psychiatry, 38,* 381–389.

Robins, L., Helzer, J., Weissman, M., Orvaschel, H., Grueberg, E., Burke, J. & Regier, D. (1984). Lifetime prevalence of specific psychiatric disorders in three cities. *Archives of General Psychiatry, 41,* 949–958.

Rogers, C. (1951). *Client-centred Therapy.* Boston: Houghton Mifflin.

Rogler, L. & Hollingshead, A. (1965). *Trapped: Families and Schizophrenia.* NY: Wiley.

Rogler, L., Malgady, R. & Rodriguea, O. (1989). *Hispanics and Mental Health: A Framework for Research.* Malabar, FL: Krieger.

Rosenhan, D. (1973). On being sane in insane places. *Science*, *179*(4070), 250–258.

Rosenhan, D. & Seligman, M. (1984). *Abnormal Psychology*. NY: W.W. Norton.

Ross, C. (1989). *Multiple Personality Disorder: Diagnosis, Clinical Features and Treatment*. NY: Wiley.

Ross, C. (1995). *Satanic Ritual Abuse: Principles of Treatment*. Toronto: University of Toronto Press.

Ross, C. (1997). *Dissociative Identity Disorder: Diagnosis, Clinical Features, and Treatment of Multiple Personality*. NY: Wiley.

Ross, C., Anderson, G., Fleisher, W. & Norton, G. (1991). The frequency of multiple personality disorder among psychiatric inpatients. *American Journal of Psychiatry*, *148*, 1717–1720.

Ross, C., Norton, G. & Wozney, K. (1989). Multiple personality disorder: An analysis of 236 cases. *Canadian Journal of Psychiatry*, *34*, 413–418.

Ross, C., Ryan, L., Vaught, L. & Eide, L. (1992). High and low dissociators in a college population. *Dissociation*, *4*, 147–151.

Ross, D.R. (1992). Discussion: An agnostic viewpoint on multiple personality disorder. *Psychoanalytic Enquiry*, *12*(1), 124–138.

Roy, C., Choudhuri, A. & Irvine, D. (1970). The prevalence of mental disorders among Saskatchewan Indians. *Journal of Cross-cultural Psychology*, *1*(4), 383–392.

Rubel, A.J. (1977). The epidemiology of a folk illness: Susto in Hispanic America. In D. Landy (ed) *Culture, Disease and Healing: Studies in Medical Anthropology*. NY: MacMillan.

Rubel, A., O'Nell, C. & Collado, R. (1985). The folk illness called susto. In R. Simons & C. Hughes (eds) *The Culture-bound Syndromes: Folk Illnesses of Psychiatric and Anthropological Interest*. Dordrecht: D. Reidel.

Saks, E. (1994). Integrating multiple personalities, murder and the status of alters as persons. *Public Affairs Quarterly*, *8*, 169–182.

Sampath, H. (1974). Prevalence of psychiatric disorders in a Southern Baffin Island Eskimo settlement. *Canadian Psychiatric Association Journal*, *19*, 363–367.

Sanders, B. & Giolas, M. (1991). Dissociation and childhood trauma in psychologically disturbed adolescents. *American Journal of Psychiatry*, *148*, 50–54.

Sanders, E., Pickrell, J. & Loftus, E. (1999). *Childhood Memories are Easily Altered.* http:/mentalhelp.net/articles/memory2.htm.

Sartorius, N., Jablensky, A., Korten, A., Ernberg, G., Anker, M., Cooper, J. & Day, R. (1986). Early manifestations and first-contact incidence of schizophrenia in different cultures: A preliminary report. *Psychological Medicine, 16,* 909–928.

Sartorius, N. et al. (1995). Progress toward achieving a common language in psychiatry II. *American Journal of Psychiatry, 152,* 1427–1437.

Schacter, D., Kihlstrom, J., Kihlstrom, L. & Berren, M. (1989). Autobiographical memory in a case of multiple personality. *Journal of Abnormal Psychology, 98,* 508–514.

Schaechter, F. (1965). Previous history of mental illness in female migrant patients admitted to the psychiatric hospital. *Royal Park Medical Journal of Australia, 2,* 277–279.

Scheff, T. (1966). *Being Mentally Ill: A Sociological Theory.* Chicago: Aldine.

Scheper-Hughes, N. (1979). *Saints, Scholars and Schizophrenics.* Berkeley: University of California Press.

Schreiber, F. (1973). *Sybil.* NY: Warner.

Seligman, M. (1973). Fall into hopelesness. *Psychology Today, 7,* 43–47.

Shapiro, S., Skinner, E., Kessler, L., Von Korff, M., German, P., Tischler, G., Leaf, P., Benham, L., Cottler, L. & Regier, D. (1984). Utilization of health and mental health services: Three epidemiological catchment area sites. *Archives of General Psychiatry, 41,* 971–978.

Simons, R. (1985). The resolution of the latah paradox. In R. Simons & C. Hughes (eds) *The Culture-bound Syndromes: Folk Illnesses of Psychiatric and Anthropological Interest.* Dordrecht: D. Reidel.

Simons, R. & Hughes, C. (eds) (1985). *The Culture-bound Syndromes: Folk Illnesses of Anthropological and Psychiatric Interest.* Dordrecht: D. Reidel.

Simpson, M. (1995). Gullible's travels, or the importance of being multiple. In L. Cohen et al. (eds) *Dissociative Identity Disorder.* Northvale, NJ: Aronson.

Simpson, R. & Halpin, G. (1986). Agreement between parents and teachers in using the revised behaviour problem checklist. *Behaviour Disorders, 12*(1), 54–58.

Singh, G. (1985). Dhat syndrome revisited. *Indian Journal of Psychiatry, 27,* 119–121.

Skinner, B.F. (1938). *Science and Behaviour.* NY: Macmillan.

Slovenko, R. (1989). The multiple personality: A challenge to legal concepts. *Journal of Psychiatry and Law, 17,* 681–715.

Slovenko, R. (1993). The multiple personality and the criminal law. *Medicine and Law, 12,* 329–340.

Smith, D. & Dumont, F. (1995). A cautionary study: Unwarranted interpretations of the Draw – a person test. *Professional Psychology: Research and Practice, 26,* 298–303.

Spaccarelli, S. (1994). Stress, appraisal and coping in child sexual abuse: A theoretical and empirical review. *Psychological Bulletin, 116,* 340–362.

Spanos, N. (1978). Witchcraft in histories of psychiatry: A critical appraisal and an alternative conceptualisation. *Psychological Bulletin, 35,* 417–439.

Spanos, N. (1994). Multiple identity enactments and multiple personality disorder: A sociocognitive perspective. *Psychological Bulletin, 116*(1), 143–165.

Spanos, N., Weekes, J. & Bertrand, L. (1985). Multiple personality: A social psychological perspective. *Journal of Abnormal Psychology, 94,* 362–376.

Spiegel, D. (1994). Dissociative disorders. In R. Hales et al. (eds) *The American Psychiatric Press Textbook of Psychiatry.* Washington, DC: APA.

Spielberger, C. (1983). *State-trait Anxiety Inventory (Form Y) Manual.* Palo Alto, CA: Consulting Psychologists' Press.

Spitzer, R., Williams, J., Kass, F. & Davies, M. (1989). National field trial of the DSM III diagnostic criteria for self-defeating personality disorder. *American Journal of Psychiatry, 146,* 1561–1567.

Spitzer, R. et al. (eds) (1994). *DSM IV Casebook.* Washington, DC: APA.

Srole, L. et al. (1962). *Mental Health in the Metropolis: The Midtown Manhattan Study.* NY: McGraw-Hill.

Staley, D. & Wand, R. (1995). Obsessive-compulsive disorder: A review of the cross-cultural epidemiological literature. *Transcultural Psychiatric Research Review, 32,* 103–136.

Sternberg, R. (1985). *Beyond IQ: A Triarchic Theory of Human Intelligence.* Cambridge: Cambridge University Press.

Strakowski, S. et al. (1995). The effects of race on diagnosis and disposition from a psychiatric emergency service. *Journal of Clinical Psychiatry*, *56*(3), 101–107.

Sue, S. (1988) Psychotherapeutic services for ethnic minorities. *American Psychologist*, *43*(4), 301–308.

Sue, S. (2000). *Ethnic/language Minorities in the Mental Health System*. Paper given at 'Visibility and invisibility' conference, Leeds, 13–14 April.

Sue, S., Fujino, D., Hu, L., Takeuchi, D. & Zane, N. (1991). Community mental health services for ethnic minority groups: A test of the cultural responsiveness hypothesis. *Journal of Consulting and Clinical Psychology*, *59*, 533–540.

Szasz, T. (1960). The myth of mental illness. *American Psychologist*, *15*, 113–118.

Szasz, T. (1962). *The Myth of Mental Illness*. NY: Harper & Row.

Szasz, T. (1971). *The Manufacture of Madness*. London: Routledge.

Taylor, C. et al. (1996). A comparison of the background of first time and repeated overdose patients. *Journal of Accidents and Emergency Medicine*, *11*(4), 238–242.

Taylor, W. & Martin, M. (1944). Multiple personality. *Journal of Abnormal and Social Psychology*, *39*, 281–300.

Thigpen, C. & Cleckley, H. (1954). *The Three Faces of Eve*. Kingsport, TN: Kingsport Press.

Thigpen, C. & Cleckley, H. (1984). On the incidence of multiple personality disorder. *International Journal of Clinical and Experimental Hypnosis*, *32*, 63–66.

Tobin, J. (1996) A case of Koro in a 20-year-old Irish male. *Irish Journal of Psychological Medicine*, *13*, (2) 72–73.

Tsai, G., Condie, D., Wu, M. & Chang, I. (1999). Functional magnetic resonance imaging of personality switches in a woman with dissociative identity disorder. *Harvard Review of Psychiatry*, *7*, 119.

Tseng, W. et al. (1990). Multi-cultural study of minor psychiatric disorders in Asia. *International Journal of Social Psychiatry*, *36*, 252–264.

Tseng, W. et al. (1992). Diagnostic patterns of social phobia: Comparison in Tokyo and Hawaii. *Journal of Nervous and Mental Disease*, *180*, 380–385.

Tseng, W. et al. (1995). Psychotherapy for the Chinese: Cultural considerations. In T. Lin et al. (eds) *Chinese Societies and Mental Health*. NY: Oxford University Press.

Turner, R. & Wagonfeld, M. (1967). Occupational mobility and schizophrenia. *American Sociological Review, 32*, 104–113.

Tyrer, P. & Steinberg, D. (1987). *Models for Mental Disorder*. London: Wiley.

Ulusahin, A. et al. (1994). A cross-cultural comparative study of depressive symptoms in British and Turkish clinical samples. *Social Psychiatry and Psychiatric Epidemiology, 29*, 31–39.

Umbenhauer, S. & DeWitte, L. (1978). Patient race and social class: Attitudes and decisions among three groups of mental health professionals. *Comprehensive Psychiatry, 19*(6), 509–515.

Unger, R. (1984). *Passion: An Essay on Personality*. NY: Free Press.

US Department of Health and Human Services (1996). *Executive Summary of the Third National Incidence Study of Child Abuse and Neglect (NIS-3)*. Washington, DC: US Department of Health and Human Services.

Ussher, J. & Dewberry, C. (1995). The nature and long-term effects of childhood sexual abuse: A survey of adult women survivors in Britain. *British Journal of Clinical Psychology, 34*, 177–192.

Vanderlinden, J. et al. (1991). Dissociative experiences in the general population in the Netherlands: A study with the Dissociative Questionnaire (DIS-Q). *Dissociation, 4*, 180–184.

Varma, V., Bouri, M. & Wig, N. (1981). Multiple personality in India: Comparison with hysterical possession state. *American Journal of Psychotherapy, 35*(1), 113–120.

Wakefield, H. & Underwager, R. (1992). Recovered memories of alleged sexual abuse: Lawsuits against parents. *Behavioural Sciences and the Law, 10*, 483–507.

Walker, C., Bonner, B. & Kaufman, K. (1988). *The Physically and Sexually Abused Child*. NY: Pergamon Press.

Warner, R. (1985). *Recovery from Schizophrenia: Psychiatry and Political Economy*. NY: Routledge.

Waxler, N. (1979). Is outcome for schizophrenia better in nonindustrialised societies? The case of Sri Lanka. *Journal of Nervous and Mental Disease, 167*, 144–158.

Weidman, H. (1979). Falling out: A diagnostic and treatment problem viewed from a transcultural perspective. *Social Science and Medicine, 13*, 95–112.

Weiss, M. (1995). Eating disorders and disordered eating in different cultures. *Psychiatric Clinics of North America, 18*, 537–553.

Weissman, M. & Klerman, G. (1981). Sex differences and the epidemiology of depression. In E. Howell & M. Bayes (eds) *Women and Mental Health*. NY: Basic Books.

Weisz, J., Suwanlert, S., Chaiyasit, W. & Walter, B. (1987). Over- and undercontrolled referral problems among children and adolescents from Thailand and the United States. *Journal of Consulting and Clinical Psychology, 55*, 719–726.

Westermayer, J. & Wintrob, D. (1978). Folk diagnosis in rural Laos. *British Journal of Psychiatry, 133*, 529–541.

Whiting, B. & Edwards, C. (1988). *Children of Different Worlds: The Formation of Social Behaviour*. Cambridge, MA: Harvard University Press.

Whitton, A., Warner, R. & Appleby, L. (1996). The pathway to care in post-natal depression. *British Journal of General Practice, 46*(408), 427–428.

WHO (1973). *International Pilot Study of Schizophrenia*. Geneva: WHO.

WHO (1977). *Apartheid and Mental Health Care*. Geneva: WHO.

WHO (1979). Schizophrenia: An international Follow-up Study. Geneva: WHO.

WHO (1983) *Depressive Disorders in Different Cultures*. Geneva: WHO.

WHO (1992, 1996). *The ICD-10 Classification of Mental and Behavioural Disorders*. Geneva: WHO.

Wilkinson, R. (1996). *Unhealthy Societies: The Afflictions of Inequality*. London: Routledge.

Williams, J. et al. (1993). *Purchasing Effective Mental Health Services for Women: A Framework for Action*. Centre for the Applied Psychology of Social Care, University of Kent at Canterbury, UK.

Williams, L. (1994). Recall of childhood trauma: A prospective study of women's memories of child sexual abuse. *Journal of Consulting and Clinical Psychology, 62*(6), 1167–1176.

Wyatt, G. (1985). The sexual abuse of Afro-American and white American women in childhood. *Child Abuse and Neglect, 9*, 507–519.

Zeigob, L., Arnold, S. & Forehand, R. (1975). An examination of observer effects in parent–child interactions. *Child Development, 46*, 509–512.

Index